The History of Retail in 100 Objects

Plus, a glimpse of the retail future
through objects not yet invented.

EDITED BY

David Roth

This History of Retail in 100 Objects has additional **interactive features.** Here is how to access them.

Download the FREE layer App

Find and scan pages with the Layar logo

Discover and enjoy our additional interactive content

Layar is an Intel Capital portfolio company

Welcome to the History of Retail in 100 Objects

From the very first transaction, retail has always played a vital part in the fabric of life. The history of retail and social developments are inextricably linked.

Inspired by The British Museum's, History of the World in 100 Objects, I have set out to define the key objects which over time have had a profound impact on the development of retail.

Arriving at the list of 100 objects has been an enriching experience. It has generated much heated debate with many different perspectives and opinions for the inclusion or exclusion of objects.

Our list of 100 objects has been arrived at through collaboration and combining wisdoms – the wisdom of crowds and the wisdom of experts.

Using social networks around the globe we first asked for objects to be nominated.

We received thousands.

An advisory board of experts from different disciplines were invited to help shortlist the most defining objects.

A full list of the advisory board members can be found on page 150. My profound thanks to them and the other experts we called on for advice or clarification along the way.

Any errors in the contents are ours alone and not the advisory board's.

To help navigate the way through this eclectic list, a framework of time periods has been constructed and each item placed within.

Whilst some of the items placed on the timeline are obvious, others are not; some could be legitimately located in several places along their 'invention, development and impact cycle'.

Where this is the case, we have used our knowledge, observation and judgement to make the call. Retail history, as we have found out along the way, is not an exact science.

For each of the 100 objects, we have illustrated it, told its story and created an overview of what its retail impact has been.

History has a way of framing the future.

It is our belief that there will be more change in retail in the next 10 years than there has been in the past 50. In conjunction with our partners on this project, Intel and the Intel 'Futures' team, we have looked into the future to try to define what objects, not invented yet, will have a considerable impact in the years to come. We have included seven objects that shed light on where the future is going. You can see these starting on page 136.

In our continuing close collaboration with Intel, we will be developing the retail future. This is the first of more future insights to come. While the future of retail is uncertain, the one certainty is that the combination of retail, technology, creativity and understanding the changing consumer has never been so intertwined and vital for success.

I am indebted to our Intel partnership team led by Joe Jenson, Jose Avalos, Maroun Ishac, Adrian Whelan, Steve Power Brown, Megan Bednarz and to Brian David Johnson, Director, Future Casting, Interactions and Experience Research Intel.

Looking to the future. Exploring key developments through the 'Future Objects'.

A special thanks to Professor Rodney Fitch CBE, for the framing of the time periods and his invaluable help in making this project a reality, to Boni Sones OBE, for her invaluable assistance and to Amanda Harrison from our team WPP who project managed the concept.

The origins of WPP was a manufacturer of shopping baskets. Retail is in our DNA.

Today, from insights, shopper marketing, digital, retail design and implementation across the globe WPP brings its talents and resources to help brands and retailers prosper in an ever competitive retail environment. To find out more visit www.shoppermarketingstore.com

We hope that you find The History of Retail in 100 Objects and the future objects an interesting and thought provoking read.

The future is not what it used to be.

David Roth
Editor, The History of Retail in 100 Objects

CEO, The Store WPP, EMEA and Asia

droth@wpp.com // twitter: davidrothlondon

The six ages of retail

THE HISTORY OF RETAILING IS ONE OF CONSTANT EVOLUTION. THIS SHOULD BE NO SURPRISE SINCE IT IS A TRUISM THAT SUCCESSFUL RETAILING MUST ALWAYS MIRROR THE SOCIETY IT SERVES. INDEED, TO KNOW RETAILING IS TO UNDERSTAND HOW SOCIETIES AROUND THE WORLD HAVE THEMSELVES EVOLVED.

Every social and commercial development, discovery and invention, both incremental and revolutionary, historical and contemporary has contributed to this evolutionary process, for shopping simply reflects us, as we would be – from caveman to internet consumer.

Sometimes this evolution has been slow and methodical, at other times uncomfortably rapid. Changes in the shopping landscape over the last 150 years, for example, have been more transformative, than during the previous 1500! But fast or slow, this process of change is relentless and evidenced since the very beginning of mankind by five significant periods. But how best to frame a history of retailing? We have chosen 100 objects and placed them chronologically within five broad time periods.

SHOPPER AS HUNTER GATHERER

Firstly, during the long and steady evolution of mankind, we humans have been genetically engineered, hard wired to find and acquire, beginning with us foraging and scavenging as hunter/gatherer societies for the very means of existence; then evolving from the hunting and gathering of simple 'needs' to more complicated gathering strategies for 'wants'. This anthropological model has been carried down through the ages and remains the template for men and women shopping today – ignored at the seller's risk!

NEOLITHIC SHOPPER

The innovations in, and subsequent formalisation of agriculture during the Neolithic Period, some 8,000 years ago, provide the platform for the second evolutionary and giant step for humanity and shopping.

Once hunter/gatherer societies became efficient, settled agriculturists, developing agri tools, domesticating animals etc., then resources could be employed outside of a survival agenda and humankind could move on to produce surpluses for sale or exchange. This, in turn, generated an infrastructure of distribution and trading centres from which a merchant class emerged. That process which today we call product specialisation, supply chain and globalisation had begun.

MONEY

Trade (the production and distribution of agricultural produce and made goods) in the then developing world, grew rapidly. Much of this trade was conducted by the barter system, but as a greater diversity of goods became available and therefore tradeable, another value method was needed. Hence the introduction of 'money' which in its various forms is the foundation for our third retail era. Money in the form of coins, beads, shells or cuneiform and much else, became the recognised liquidity fuelling trade and the subsequent shopping experience. And it is money, as a universal medium of exchange, which has evolved as the oxygen of the entire retail experience.

Pre-history

Cave Man

8,000 to 2,000 BC

Neolithic Period

2,000 BC to 1600

Early Trading

A GLIMPSE OF THE RETAIL FUTURE THROUGH OBJECTS NOT YET INVENTED/ COMMERCIALISED

MODERN SHOPPING

In the great sweep of social and retail history, the 'modern' shopping experience can be said to have commenced with the appearance of the department store in the middle of the 19th century. For the first time, thousands of disparate goods could be gathered together and shopped for at a single destination. Early forms of entertainment and hospitality were woven into the format so that shopping as a leisure activity became a part of the shopping experience. Since then format has followed format – from department store to supermarket to shopping centre and hypermarket with much else in between.

And now, online and digital shopping enabled by the internet which will utterly transform the retail landscape and dramatically change the citizen consumers role within it.

CONCLUSION

Constant change is the very nature of retailing, made manifest by the objects invented or embraced by retailing to facilitate, improve and deliver an appropriate shopping experience to society, which is itself the magna of this change. "Lock up a department store today, reopen it in 100 years' time and you will have a ready-made museum!" claimed Andy Warhol 50 years ago. That is as true today as when he said it – the question is, will there even be department stores in 50 years' time? Maybe not, but shopping and retail objects – always!!

MASS PRODUCTION

The inventions, innovations and entrepreneurship of the Industrial Revolution in the two centuries between 1700 and 1900 had a profound effect on the social and retail landscape, transforming it forever. Industrialisation brought into existence inexpensive, mass-produced commodities and products, previously unavailable to a majority. The distribution of these new products required a new retail approach, which brought into existence speciality shops, urban galleria and department stores.

As the new specialised , better-organised retail formats emerged, steadily replacing the informal market trader, these new 'shopkeepers' as they became known, employed shop fronts with their proprietor's name above the door – trust and brand identity had been born.

1700 to 1900

18th and 19th Centuries

1901 to NOW

20th and 21st Centuries

2013-2023

The Future

CAVE MAN

ANIMAL SKIN

40,000 years ago
CAVE PAINTINGS
Cave paintings show that people in that time period planned out hunts, had a sense of self image and self-importance, communicated abstract concepts, had the beginnings of a mythology.

NEOLITHIC

8,000 to 2,000 BC
ORIGINS OF AGRICULTURE
The main advantage of agriculture, is that it allows to grow food, while you stay in a permanent place. Together with livestock, agriculture makes hunting unnecessary. That allowed the appearance of permanent settlements.

SHELF

ROYAL EXCHANGE

IN-STORE GRAPHIC

ABACUS

BALANCE SCALES

CUNEIFORM TABLET

MARKET

LEDGER

SIGNAGE

COWRIE SHELL

PAPER MONEY

COIN

GREEK AGORA

MIRROR

FOIRE SAINT-GERMAIN, PARIS

RIALTO BRIDGE

CHALKBOARD

GAS LIGHT

PRICE TAG

CHAIN STORE

GALARIES DU BOIS

PRICE TAG

DEPARTMENT STORE

POCKET BALANCE

20TH & 21ST CENTURY

ALLEN KEY

SELFRIDGE'S LAVATORY

FLOAT GLASS

PLASTIC PACKAGING

NEON LIGHTING

SHOPPING BAG

CALCULATOR

DELIVERY VAN

CHECKOUT

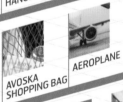

SUPERMARKET

ESCALATOR

AIR CONDITIONING

CLOTHES HANGER

TANNOY

SHOPPING CENTRE

CONVEYOR BELT

COMPUTER

CREDIT CARD

KVASS BARREL

AVOSKA SHOPPING BAG

AEROPLANE

CCTV

DISCOUNT STORE

PRICE GUN

SHOPPING TROLLEY

HIGH STREET
(BOOK BY JM RICHARDS & ERIC RAVILIOUS 1938)

FLUORESCENT TUBE

RATION BOOK

PALLET

SPECIALITY STORE

TUPPERWARE

PLANOGRAM

RFID

1981: PC LAUNCHED BY IBM
featuring Intel 8088 processor.

1969: MOON LANDING
The Space Race sparked unprecedented increases in spending on education and pure research, which accelerated scientific advancements and led to beneficial spin-off technologies.

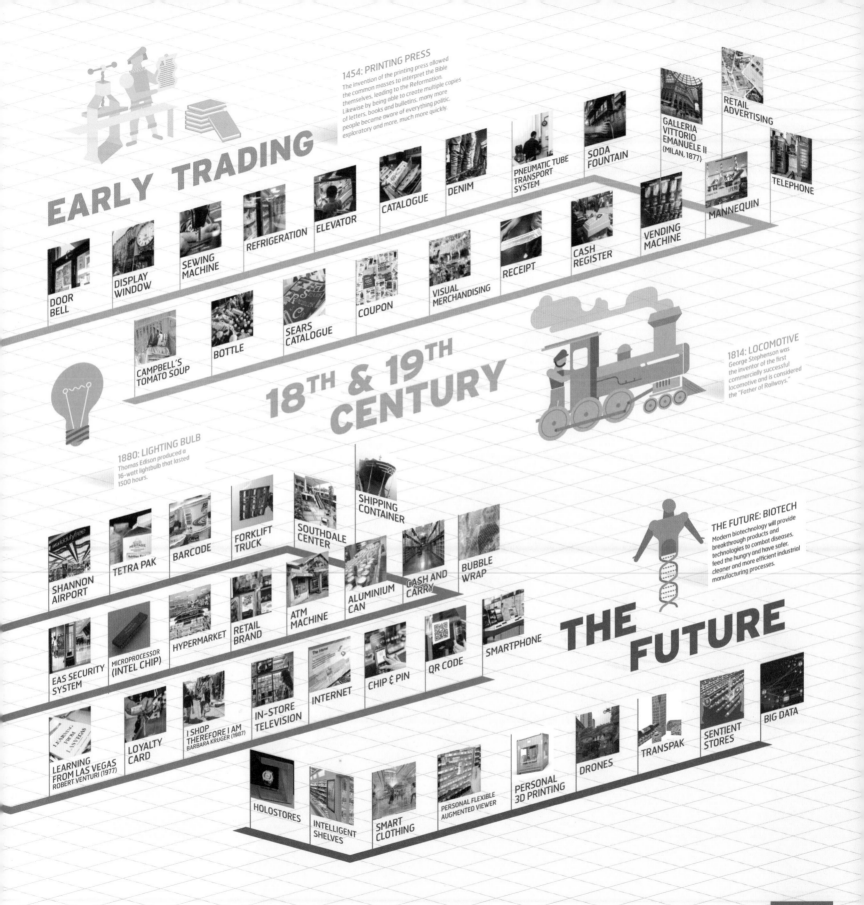

EARLY TRADING

1454: PRINTING PRESS
The invention of the printing press allowed the common masses to interpret the Bible themselves, leading to the Reformation. Likewise by being able to create multiple copies of letters, books and bulletins, many more people became aware of everything politic, exploratory and more, much more quickly.

RETAIL ADVERTISING

GALLERIA VITTORIO EMANUELE II (MILAN, 1877)

TELEPHONE

SODA FOUNTAIN

PNEUMATIC TUBE TRANSPORT SYSTEM

DENIM

CATALOGUE

ELEVATOR

REFRIGERATION

SEWING MACHINE

DISPLAY WINDOW

DOOR BELL

VENDING MACHINE

MANNEQUIN

CASH REGISTER

RECEIPT

VISUAL MERCHANDISING

COUPON

SEARS CATALOGUE

BOTTLE

CAMPBELL'S TOMATO SOUP

18TH & 19TH CENTURY

1814: LOCOMOTIVE
George Stephenson was the inventor of the first commercially successful locomotive and is considered the "Father of Railways."

1880: LIGHTING BULB
Thomas Edison produced a 16-watt lightbulb that lasted 1500 hours.

SHIPPING CONTAINER

SOUTHDALE CENTER

FORKLIFT TRUCK

BARCODE

TETRA PAK

SHANNON AIRPORT

BUBBLE WRAP

CASH AND CARRY

ALUMINIUM CAN

ATM MACHINE

RETAIL BRAND

HYPERMARKET

MICROPROCESSOR (INTEL CHIP)

EAS SECURITY SYSTEM

SMARTPHONE

QR CODE

CHIP & PIN

INTERNET

IN-STORE TELEVISION

I SHOP THEREFORE I AM BARBARA KRUGER (1987)

LOYALTY CARD

LEARNING FROM LAS VEGAS ROBERT VENTURI (1977)

THE FUTURE

THE FUTURE: BIOTECH
Modern biotechnology will provide breakthrough products and technologies to combat diseases, feed the hungry and have safer, cleaner and more efficient industrial manufacturing processes.

BIG DATA

SENTIENT STORES

TRANSPAK

DRONES

PERSONAL 3D PRINTING

PERSONAL FLEXIBLE AUGMENTED VIEWER

SMART CLOTHING

INTELLIGENT SHELVES

HOLOSTORES

1

SHOPPER AS HUNTER GATHERER

Animal Skin

ANIMAL SKINS ARE USED TO CREATE A WIDE RANGE OF CONSUMER PRODUCTS TODAY, BUT IN EARLIER TIMES THEY PLAYED A MORE VITAL ROLE IN THE FACILITATION OF COMMERCE. ANIMAL SKINS CREATED GREAT WEALTH AND FUELLED THE DEVELOPMENT AND GROWTH OF ONE OF THE WORLD'S GREATEST RETAILERS AND MOST RECOGNISABLE LUXURY BRANDS.

Mankind has made extensive use of animal skins throughout history for all manner of clothing and shelter and to create a wide range of products. Animal skins were essential for much of man's existence and very survival which in turn made them extremely valuable to early peoples. Animal skins often served as a form of crude currency that could be exchanged for other goods. In some cases, animal skins such has deer hide were refined into a type of currency that preceded the development of paper money.

Over time, the utility of animal skins as a form of currency waned, but they gained greater relevance to society as symbols of wealth and status and a raw material for mass-produced consumer goods. New processes and manufacturing techniques allowed animal skins to be transformed into a wide range of consumer products prized for their durability, texture and versatility. Animal skins also fuelled the development of global luxury brands for which manufacturers were able to command premium prices.

Animal skins long ago ceased playing a role as an instrument of trade or currency, but they remain highly prized throughout the world – so much so that extreme measures are now taken to protect select species threatened with extinction.

Advancements in the development of synthetic animal hides have made them indistinguishable from the real thing and a viable alternative in many cases.

Contribution to Retail History

Animal skins served a variety of roles, but the enduring impact on the retail industry was to give rise to the Hudson's Bay Company in 1670. The harvesting of animal skins that were abundant throughout North America enabled the company to control fur trading for several centuries and accumulate vast wealth. That wealth was transformed into a retail business. For a period of time the Hudson's Bay Company was one of the world's largest and most influential retail operations.

2

8,000 to 2,000 BC

NEOLITHIC
SHOPPER

TRADERS HAVE ALWAYS NEEDED COUNTING BOARDS OF SOME KIND. THE EARLIEST VERSIONS, WHICH PREDATED THE ABACUS, WOULD HAVE BEEN USED BY TRADERS AT MARKETS. TRADERS DREW LINES IN THE SAND WITH THEIR FINGERS OR A STYLUS OF SOME KIND. THEY WOULD THEN PLACE PEBBLES BETWEEN THOSE LINES TO REPRESENT NUMBERS.

Abacus

Contribution to Retail History

As the first known calculating mechanism, the abacus enabled merchants and traders to add, subtract, multiply and divide without the use of pebbles, twigs or other 'representations'. Being liberated to work on larger, more complex calculations was a significant advancement in the earliest days of retail management.

THE ABACUS - OR COUNTING FRAME - EVOLVED FROM ANCIENT TIMES, THROUGH TO THE MIDDLE AGES AND MODERN TIMES. IN 500 BC THE EARLY COUNTING BOARDS INCLUDED THE SALAMIS TABLET, THE ROMAN CALCULI AND THE HAND-ABACUS. THE ROMAN HAND ABACUS WAS OFTEN MADE FROM STONE AND METAL.

In the Middle Ages came the Apices, the coin-board, and the Line-board, which date from 5 AD to around 1400 AD.

Most were made from wood, and originally the beads on which you counted ran vertically. By the time the system had evolved to Line-boards, the columns ran horizontally.

From 1200 AD the abacus evolved into the Chinese suan-pan, the Japanese soroban, and the Russian schoty. The classic Chinese abacus is the one we are most familiar with. It has two beads on the upper deck and 5 on the lower deck, and is often called the

'2/5' abacus. From about 1850 this was replaced with the '1/5' abacus, with one bead on the top deck and five beads on the bottom deck.

The Chinese abacus was further adapted by Lee Kai-Chen, and by 1958 the 'new' abacus could be found in use, complete with an instruction book. It has more decks top and bottom combining the 1/4 soroban model and the 2/5 suan-pan style. Kai-Chen said it was a "Revolution of Chinese Calculators".

Balance Scales

BALANCE SCALES WERE IN USE IN MESOPOTAMIA AS EARLY AS AROUND THE YEAR 4000 BC. THEY WERE PROBABLY DERIVED FROM THE PRINCIPLES OF A YOKE, WHEREBY TWO EQUAL WEIGHTS WOULD BALANCE IF SUSPENDED EITHER SIDE OF A CENTRAL BEAM.

EARLY BALANCE SCALES MEASURE RELATIVE WEIGHT (AS OPPOSED TO ACTUAL WEIGHT). MEASURES WERE CALCULATED BY PUTTING THE OBJECT MEASURED ON ONE PLATE, AND STONES (THE COUNTER-WEIGHT) ON THE OTHER, UNTIL EQUILIBRIUM WAS REACHED.

In the late 18th century, a way to measure absolute weight was developed by Richard Salter when he invented the spring scale. This calculated the weight of an item by measuring the pressure it registered when hung by a hook attached to the spring.

Around the same period (in 1897), one of the first commercial price-indicating scales was being developed in America. A weighed cursor, graduated vertically into prices per pound, was slid along a steelyard, which is a device with a short arm taking the item to be weighed, and a long graduated arm along which a weight is moved until it balances. The price of the goods could be read off the chart at the point where balance was achieved. Slow to actually provide a reading, it failed to catch on.

From the 1940s, scales were incorporating electronic devices to make them more accurate. Today, the traditional balance scales so associated with grocers, butchers, confectioners and a myriad of other retailers, have been replaced almost entirely by digital scales. These scales not only weigh to a tenth of a gram, but by communicating with the retailer's pricing system also print labels, instantly giving the weight and associated price of each weighed purchase. Scales are also integrated into supermarket checkouts, greatly streamlining the process.

Contribution to Retail History

Scales are one of civilisations most important developments. For centuries, traders have bought and sold goods according to weight and today all trade depends on having a fair system of weights and measures controlled by law. The food we eat and many of the products we use will have been weighed and measured – probably many times – in their journey through the supply chain. Without the ability to measure weight and ascribe a value to it, commerce would not have progressed beyond the basic bartering system. Thus, the scales became the principle way of determining the cost of an item, and a cornerstone of retailing as we know it.

Cuneiform Tablet

CIVILISATION'S NEED TO WRITE THINGS DOWN, MAKE A LIST, KEEP A RECORD, CATEGORISE DATA AND THEREBY PAY TAXES, GOES BACK TO THE EARLIEST TIMES. THE FIRST SYSTEM OF WRITING USED TO RECORD THIS INFORMATION (THAT IS KNOWN TO US) IS CALLED 'CUNEIFORM SCRIPT'.

CUNEIFORM USED PICTORIAL SYMBOLS SET OUT IN COLUMNS ON CLAY TABLETS, USING A BLUNT REED FOR A STYLUS. THE BLUNT REEDS LEFT A 'WEDGE SHAPED' IMPRESSION, AND THIS IS WHERE THE NAME CUNEIFORM COMES FROM, THE LATIN FOR 'WEDGE'.

This writing system began in Sumer, in Mesopotamia, as long ago as 8000 BC. The early tablets were in their simplest form principally used for record keeping — agrarian inventories for grain, animals and equipment.

But as the ancient world increasingly urbanised, these writings took on a more commercial form and were employed to record bargains sealed, ships' cargoes, and lists of manufactured goods.

Early Sumerians used cuneiform to list the clay tokens they used to exchange and store their agricultural and manufactured goods. The clay tokens were put in clay containers and they impressed onto the sealed containers, one picture for each token inside the container. As time passed, it became a standard practice for the major cities to date documents by year, names, and their respective kings. It also became a way of calculating how much people should pay in taxes.

These early writings in turn led to their use for everyday purposes, not least in shopping. Dr Irvine Finkel, of the British Museum and noted Cuneiform scholar, has established that some of the earliest tablets he has examined are shopping lists!

Contribution to Retail History

Cuneiform tablets highlight our shopping journey from the ancient world to modern times. The shopping bag and the shopping list have survived the journey of time and civilisations. Both have been in use for millennia and whilst we have little evidence of an ancient bag, it is interesting to see from the many clay tablets that have survived, that the ancients wrote out their lists just as we do today.

Market

THE PRINCIPLE OF THE MARKET IS AS OLD AS CIVILIZATION ITSELF. MARKETS AND MARKET PLACES ARE STILL TO BE FOUND EVERYWHERE, AND EACH COUNTRY HAS ITS OWN TRADITIONS AND CUSTOMS.

In China, every neighbourhood has its own little vegetable and meat market, selling local produce. These Chinese markets are a focus of activity and noise, and modern Chinese supermarkets still reflect the look and feel of these original markets with stores housing 'mini' markets and stalls within them.

In Moscow, 21% of all retail trade takes place in markets and indeed markets continue to occupy a special place in the hearts and minds of Russian shoppers. About half of all clothes and shoes sold in Russia are brought at markets – the prices are cheaper and sometimes the goods are newer and more plentiful than in retail outlets. Although perishable goods are also offered, grocery retailing has expanded significantly to the extent that now only about 11% of all food is sold at markets.

For centuries, across every part of India, weekly Haats or 'gatherings' would see vendors gathering in market places. As towns and cities grew, small retail stores began stocking more goods, and high street bazaars were formed where traders sold a range of goods, food, and perishables.

In 1869, the Mumbai Crawford Market could be said to be the first form of shopping centre in India, then in 1874, the Hogg Market was built in Calcutta. Now known as the New Market, it was designed by an East Indian Railways Architect, R.R. Banya, and named after the municipal commissioner of Calcutta, Sir Stuart Hogg. The Hogg Market had a garden, a red brick Gothic clock tower and benches for shoppers to rest upon.

Just a decade ago the majority of Indian shoppers still relied on street markets. But shopping traditions here are changing too. The street markets are still appreciated for their colourful displays and merchandise, but new shopping malls offering entertainment and experiences for all the family are also attracting many customers through their doors. Retailing is now the largest private industry in India and the second largest employer after agriculture.

Contribution to Retail History

Markets have existed throughout human history. Often centrally located or in an area of optimum footfall – at a port or roadside – wherever buyers and sellers could get together a market could be created. The focus of economic activity for the surrounding area, markets were also and remain today, a focus for social events, customs and traditions.

Shelf

THE SHELF IS A FUNDAMENTAL COMPONENT OF THE STORE EXPERIENCE AND ALLOWS RETAILERS TO DISPLAY PRODUCTS AND ENCOURAGE SALES, IMPART INFORMATION AND DELIVER PROMOTIONAL INCENTIVES. THE TYPE AND QUALITY OF MATERIALS USED IN THE FABRICATION OF SHELVES CONTRIBUTES TO PERCEPTIONS OF THE RETAILER AND THE PRODUCTS OFFERED FOR SALE.

SHELVES WERE CREATED IN ANCIENT TIMES OUT OF A DESIRE TO ELEVATE AND PROTECT VALUABLE OBJECTS, WHICH AT THE TIME TENDED TO BE SCROLLS OR OTHER TYPES OF WRITTEN DOCUMENTS.

Advancements in printing which made the publication of books possible meant libraries needed extensive shelving for storage.

The application of shelves was readily apparent to retailers who equipped stores with horizontal surfaces to store products in back rooms and display products to customers so they could easily be retrieved by clerks.

The boom years for shelves arrived with the birth of self-service shopping in department stores in the 1800s and later in supermarkets. The new approach to retail meant shoppers needed to be able to see and touch products and shelves were the solution.

Shelving materials can consist of wood, metal, glass, plastic, stone or composite materials and come in an endless array of finishes. Shelves perform the most basic of functions within a retail environment, but the combination of materials, finishes and configurations present retailers with an infinite number of options when it comes to creatively merchandising a store.

In addition to their important contribution to merchandising, shelves play an important role in supply chain management. Different categories require specific shelving solutions which can vary widely from car batteries and cans of paint to folded shirts and delicate ceramics. Shelf design must account for the unique characteristics of each, to enable effective merchandising while providing adequate holding capacity to maintain acceptable in-stock levels based on anticipated rates of sale and the retailer's replenishment capabilities.

An amazing array of shelving is evident in the retail industry today.

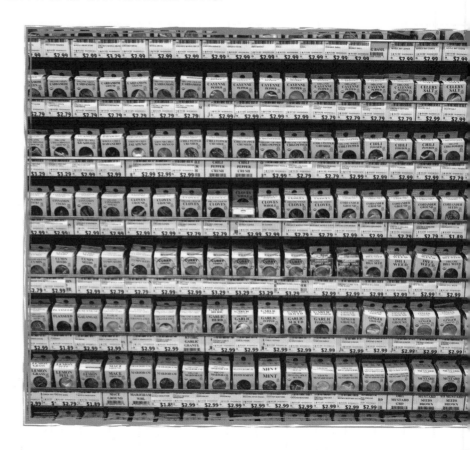

Contribution to Retail History

Early shelving options allowed retailers to increase the inventory capacity of their stores and the productivity of selling space. Chain stores who made use of consistent shelving configurations were able to optimise product assortments and increase sales. The extensive range of shelving materials, finishes and configurations also advanced the practice of visual merchandising which greatly affected store experience.

3

2,000 BC to 1600

EARLY TRADING AND MONEY

Cowrie Shell

IN THE EARLIEST CIVILISATIONS THE CONCEPT OF 'TRADING' WAS WELL ESTABLISHED, BUT THERE WAS NO EQUIVALENT TO MONEY FOR USE IN SUCH TRANSACTIONS.

TO GET YOUR FOOD YOU WOULD 'BARTER' AN ITEM SUCH AS FISH, FUR, CLOTHES, DECORATIVE ITEMS, TOOLS OR EVEN WEAPONS. FROM 9,000 TO 6,000 BC THE NEAREST EQUIVALENT TO CURRENCY WAS CATTLE.

Archaeological evidence suggests that the first widespread form of currency was introduced around 1200 BC, through the adoption of the cowrie shell as a trading 'token'. These shells shared many of the attributes of modern coins – being durable, portable, easily recognisable and hard to fake. As well as being counted out in payment, they could also be traded by weight.

The cowrie shell was indigenous to the Indian and Pacific Oceans, but its use as a trading token spread and it became the most commonly used means of payment across large parts of Asia, Africa, and some of the outer reaches of Europe. The significance of shell trading in China is evidenced by ancient artefacts that show simplified representations of the cowrie used as part of the characters for words with economic meaning – such as money, coin, buy.

Just as with currency exchanges today, the value of the cowrie shell could fluctuate, depending on where it was being traded. For example, in some places a few cowries would buy a cow; whereas in the Maldives (where cowrie shell collecting and trading was a big business), several hundred thousands of cowries would be required in exchange for a single gold dinar.

The Portuguese, English, French and Dutch played a significant role in promoting the cowrie as a currency for commercial transactions, including using it for trading in slaves. In Western Africa, 'shell money' remained legal tender right up until the mid 19th century.

Contribution to Retail History

As the first recognised 'common currency', the cowrie shell played a vital contribution to the development of commerce and early formal retail. Non-perishable, lightweight and robust, it opened up international trade opportunities by enabling transactions to be carried out across continents and between different cultures.

Paper Money

THE EARLIEST PAPER MONEY WAS USED IN CHINA AROUND 1000 BC AND IT WAS MOST COMMONLY USED AS A LETTER OF CREDIT, TRANSFERRED OVER LARGE DISTANCES.

IN THE 13TH CENTURY, WHEN GHENGIS KHAN CONQUERED CHINA, HE QUICKLY GRASPED THE POTENTIAL OF ITS PAPER MONEY AND BEGAN USING IT AS A CURRENCY THROUGHOUT HIS EMPIRE. HE SEIZED PEOPLE'S EXISTING SUPPLIES OF GOLD AND SILVER AND GAVE THEM PAPER CURRENCY IN EXCHANGE, LEAVING THE POPULATION NO OPTION BUT TO TRADE WITH PAPER MONEY.

Although the use of paper money spread and continued for several hundred years, it was not wholeheartedly embraced. In Persia, its introduction in 1294 led to a complete collapse of trade. In the 15th century in China, the issuing of paper notes was mismanaged, leading to rapid depreciation of their value and causing inflation. As a consequence, the use of paper money in China ceased in 1455 and did not resume for many years.

Europe came far behind Asia and the Arab world in its adoption of paper money, primarily because Europe didn't have paper until around 1100 AD. The alleged first instance of use of paper money in Europe was in Spain in 1438 during a Moorish invasion (a Spanish military leader paid his soldiers with paper).

Early on in the introduction of paper money, European governments took over its production and began printing 'official' paper money. These paper receipts were all given fixed values and people began leaving their heavy coins with merchants in exchange for them. The earliest known English goldsmith certificates were being used by 1633 as proof of ability to pay.

Nations and colonies developed their own paper money, leading to the variety of notes in use today. In 1816, governments established the 'gold standard', to ward against inflation. This tied the value of paper money to a specific amount of gold, held in the government treasuries. The US officially adopted the gold standard in 1900.

Today, not all notes are widely accepted and the average lifespan for a currency's circulation is only 39 years. The longest running paper currencies are the British pound, (introduced in 1694) and the US dollar (introduced in 1792).

Contribution to Retail History

Paper money is a promise to 'pay the bearer' a set amount and as such its success as a currency depends on mutual confidence in its validity (unlike early coins which had an intrinsic face value of their own). It was pivotal to the opening of trade between regions and nations, offering a light, easily portable alternative to the cumbersome weight of coins.

Coin

IN CHINA, FROM AROUND 1200 BC, THE COWRIE SHELL WAS USED AS AN ITEM OF EXCHANGE – 'SHELL MONEY'. ARCHAEOLOGISTS' FINDS SUGGEST THAT FROM 1000 BC THE CHINESE BEGAN TO PRODUCE MOCK COWRIE SHELLS MADE OF METAL.

HOWEVER, EVIDENCE INDICATES THAT METAL COINS ALSO APPEARED INDEPENDENTLY OF EACH OTHER AND THESE CHINESE VERSIONS, AT TWO OTHER LOCATIONS ON THE EURASIAN CONTINENT – LYDIA (NOW TURKEY) AND INDIA BETWEEN 700-600 BC. IT IS THOUGHT THAT INCREASED TRADE BETWEEN THESE LOCATIONS WAS A TRIGGER FOR THE CREATION OF COINS TO REPLACE THE BARTER SYSTEM.

Bartering had two distinct disadvantages – the person wishing to 'buy' may not have anything the 'seller' wished to acquire, and even if they could agree on a trade, the haggling process was time consuming. Coins offered a solution in that they represented fixed values and could be exchanged not for their intrinsic value, but in order to change hands again in payment for some other goods.

An appreciation of the value of metals such as gold and silver had already developed. Since these metals were durable, portable and demand for them remained constant, they were a natural choice for use as a common currency. The value of a coin depended upon its weight and metal content.

The idea of using coins quickly spread to Greece, and because the early Greeks were keen traders throughout the Mediterranean, coinage spread around the region. Alexander the Great minted vast quantities of silver coins, using them to pay his armies and keep them loyal. It is believed that this significantly contributed to his ability to expand across three continents.

Contribution to Retail History

Coins increased social mobility and opened up trading opportunities between cities, nations and continents. Signifying a token of trust, with a stored value that was redeemable over time, coins enabled traders and customers to conduct a 'fair exchange' of agreed, recognised worth.

Greek Agora

BY ABOUT 600 BC ALL CITIES IN ANCIENT GREECE WOULD HAVE HAD AN AGORA NEAR THEIR CENTRE.

A MARKET PLACE AS WELL AS A MEETING PLACE, THE AGORA WAS USUALLY A RECTANGULAR SPACE SURROUNDED BY BUILDINGS AND FREQUENTED BY POLITICIANS, TRADERS, ARISTOCRATS, SCIENTISTS AND SLAVES. ALONG ONE EDGE WAS THE 'STOA', A LONG COVERED WALKWAY WITH SHOPS LOCATED IN IT, WHERE MORE EXPENSIVE ITEMS COULD BE PURCHASED THAN THOSE FOUND ON THE TRADERS' STALLS.

Farmers brought their produce to the agora and set up stalls selling meat, fish, fruits, vegetables, cheeses, eggs, honey, and wine. Cattle and grain were also traded, as were more exotic items such as gems, silks, wool, and, of course, slaves. A hive of activity, craftsmen would ply their trade and moneychangers and bankers would carry out their business. 'Shopping' at the agora was conducted by men and their household slaves, not by women.

The agora was also a focus for cultural and community activity. Political debate, theatre, and musical performances would draw citizens in as they fraternised with friends and business associates. It also served as a labour exchange as employers mixed with men looking for work. Although it was a predominantly male environment, women were allowed to use the agora's public fountains to collect water.

Contribution to Retail History

A focal point for trading and bartering, the agora is one of many examples of how even in ancient civilisations, communities instinctively drew together to share, compare, buy and sell.

Mirror

REFLECTIONS OF OUR OWN IMAGE HAD A MAGICAL SIGNIFICANCE IN ANCIENT CULTURES. IN EARLY TIMES GLASS POLISHED STONES OR METAL WERE USED. THE ROMANS COATED FLAT GLASS WITH SILVER OR GOLD FOIL.

JUSTUS VON LIEBIG DISCOVERED THE CHEMICAL PROCESS OF COATING A GLASS SURFACE WITH METALLIC SILVER IN 1835. TODAY, MIRRORS ARE STILL MADE BY COATING A THIN LAYER OF MOLTEN ALUMINIUM OR SILVER ONTO THE BACK OF A PLATE GLASS IN A VACUUM. HOWEVER, MIRRORS AND THEIR CAPABILITIES ARE STILL EVOLVING.

During the Renaissance, Nuremberg and Venice became centres of excellence for mirror production but by the middle of the 17th century mirror making was practised extensively in London and Paris. The Royal Palace of Versailles had incredible mirrors in the staterooms, which created a sensation at the time. Craftsmen such as Grinling Gibbons in the late 17th and early 18th centuries produced elaborately carved mirror frames, and English brothers Robert and James Adam created ceiling-high fireplace units that used mirrors to create a special ambiance.

As the 19th century progressed, mirror making became cheaper and mirrors were put into wardrobes, sideboards, and clothing retailers began installing them in and around store interiors and in changing and fitting rooms. Three-way mirrors were also introduced to help customers see themselves from different angles when trying on clothes.

Today, mirrors are taking on new dimensions as digital technology begins to extend their capabilities for retail use. For example, interactive mirrors in stores incorporate a camera which captures the customer's body dimensions and stance. Using hand gestures, the customer 'swipes' different outfits from a display menu and the mirror shows their reflection with the selected garment superimposed over their on-screen image. The digital delay mirror records the customer's reflection and outputs it on a two second delay, enabling them to see what they look like from the back.

Contribution to Retail History

Mirrors are key to encouraging purchase of garments as the ability to see how they look on the wearer plays a major role in the decision-making process. The fitting room is a key part of the shopper experience. Mirrors give consumers the ultimate reassurance of the validity of their purchase decision and as such help generate millions in retail sale.

Foire Saint-Germain

THERE'S BEEN AN ANNUAL FAIR AT FOIRE SAINT-GERMAIN IN PARIS SINCE 1176, AND WITH FAIRS COME TRADE AND PRODUCE.

IN 1482, LOUIS XI ESTABLISHED THE FAIRGROUND FOR THE BENEFIT OF THE ABBEY OF SAINT-GERMAIN-DES-PRES, LOCATED NEARBY. IT WAS DESTROYED BY FIRE IN MARCH 1762, BUT ROSE AGAIN FROM THE ASHES

The fair traditionally lasted from three to five weeks and was staged around Easter. During the 1700s it opened on February 3rd and closed on Palm Sunday. All kinds of exotic acts performed: tightrope walkers, animal trainers, marionette manipulators and more. It was also a great place for trading, bartering and 'raffling' of retail merchandise to the highest bidder, as recorded by Philip Skippon, a visitor to the Foire in the 1660s: "the place the fair is kept in, is a large square house with six or seven rows of shops, where customers play at dice when they come to buy things; the commodity is first bought, and then they play who shall pay for it. After candle-lighting is the greatest gaming, sometimes the king comes and dices..."

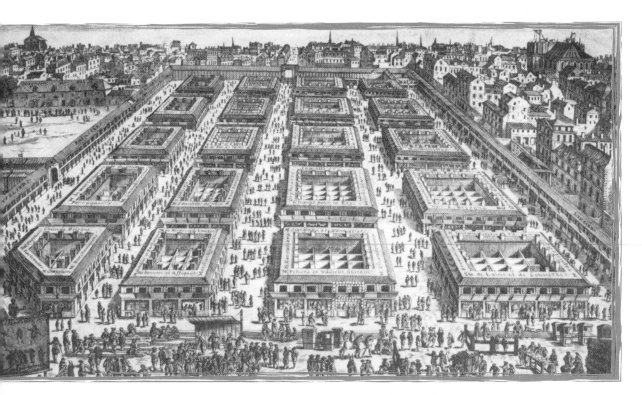

This account of raffling as a social pastime (although we would recognise it today more as a form of auctioning) is corroborated by another Englishman abroad, Martin Lister, who wrote in 1697:

"The great rendezvous is at night, after the play and opera are done; and raffling for all things vendible is the great diversion; no shop wanting two or three raffling boards. Monsieur, the Dauphin, and other princes of the blood come, at least once in the fair-time..."

Today the Saint-Germain market is covered and is still on part of the old fairground site, hosting antique fairs, pottery days, and festivals.

Contribution to Retail History

Markets and fairs the world over were the precursors to modern retailing and Foire Saint-Germain is one such example. While it may not be feasible to draw a direct line between the raffles held at Foire Saint-Germain in the mid-17th century and specific developments in retail, it is fair to reflect that the popularity of 'raffling' has, in the 21st century seen a surge in popularity with the advent of eBay.

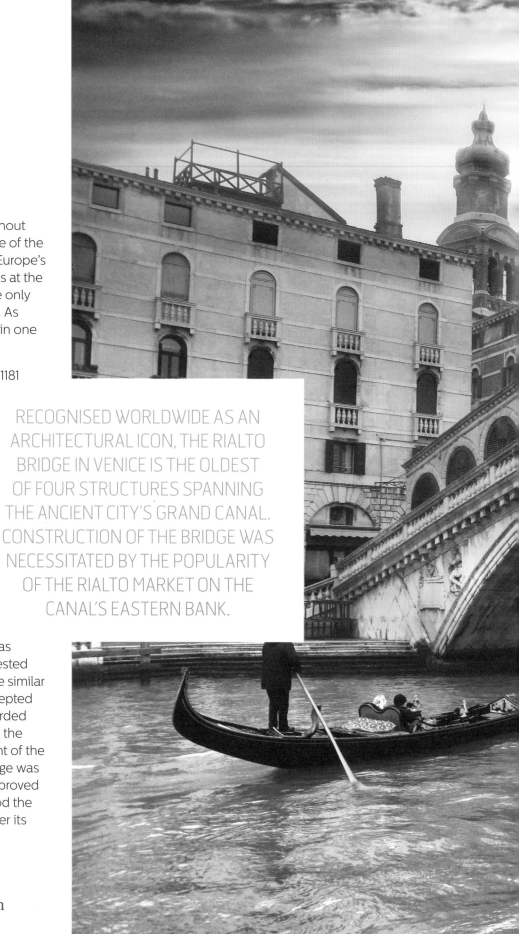

The Rialto Bridge

Venice flourished as a centre of trade throughout the 13th and 14th centuries and its dominance of the maritime industry and trade made it one of Europe's most prosperous cities. The Rialto Bridge was at the centre of it all and for centuries served as the only dry land connection across the Grand Canal. As such, the bridge helped facilitate commerce in one of the world's most vibrant trading hubs.

An early version of the bridge established in 1181 was made of floating pontoons. However, the establishment of the Rialto Market and its growing popularity prompted construction of a higher capacity wooden structure. The original wooden bridge was built with inclined ramps on either side and a centre section which could move to accommodate the passage of larger vessels on the canal. Although an improvement from earlier versions, the wood structure required frequent maintenance, occasionally caught fire and collapsed on several occasions.

RECOGNISED WORLDWIDE AS AN ARCHITECTURAL ICON, THE RIALTO BRIDGE IN VENICE IS THE OLDEST OF FOUR STRUCTURES SPANNING THE ANCIENT CITY'S GRAND CANAL. CONSTRUCTION OF THE BRIDGE WAS NECESSITATED BY THE POPULARITY OF THE RIALTO MARKET ON THE CANAL'S EASTERN BANK.

To remedy the situation, a stone structure was considered and in 1551 proposals were requested from architects. A design for a stone structure similar to the wooden bridge to be replace was accepted from Antonio da Ponte. The design was regarded as bold, if not foolhardy, and sceptics feared the centre span would collapse due to the weight of the stone. Construction proceeded and the bridge was completed in 1591. The concerns of sceptics proved unfounded as the Rialto Bridge has withstood the test of time and more than four centuries after its completion remains serviceable.

Contribution to Retail History

The Rialto Bridge in all its various forms contributed to the success of the Rialto Market and the establishment of Venice as a hub of global commerce. The bridge highlighted the important role infrastructure plays in facilitating commerce and provided crucial ingress and egress to the city's vibrant market. The establishment of new sea routes diminished Venice's role on the world stage, but the enduring image of the Rialto Bridge serves as a reminder of the city's bygone greatness.

Signage

EARLY STATISTICIAN GREGORY KING ESTIMATED THAT BY THE LATE 17TH CENTURY, ENGLAND AND WALES HAD ABOUT 40,000 SHOPKEEPERS. THEY HUNG SIGNS TO DISPLAY THE EMBLEMS OF THEIR TRADES AND THESE BECAME A COMMON WAY FOR TRADERS TO COMMUNICATE WITH THEIR CUSTOMERS.

WHEN RETAIL BEGAN TO EXPAND FROM OUTDOOR MARKETS TO PERMANENT PREMISES, RETAILERS (WHO OFTEN LIVED OVER THE SHOP) ALSO NEEDED A SIGN TO BE ABLE TO COMMUNICATE ONE PARTICULARLY ESSENTIAL PIECE OF INFORMATION – OPEN OR CLOSED?

In China, signs were originally used in restaurants, teahouses, drugstores, and then draperies, pawnshops, hotels and tobacconists. They were made of cloth, and later leather, bamboo, wood, aluminium, iron, copper and tin, and were hung in front of the doors showing the particular symbol of their trade. Interestingly, there are various taboos in the use of shop signs in China; signs are not 'hung up' but 'invited in' because gua (hang up) is thought to be unlucky. When a shop sign falls on the ground it is also thought to be a bad omen because the God of Wealth, held in awe by the Chinese, might not approve.

In 1389, King Richard II of England, decreed that landlords must put signs outside their inns, so that inspectors could identify and visit them; there is a record from 1393 of a publican being prosecuted for not having a sign. In 1567 and 1577, France issued similar rules. When the signs became too large for safety reasons, in Paris in 1761 and in London around the same time, laws were introduced which dictated that signs had to be placed flat against a wall or removed.

Today, retail signage is used to communicate a raft of different messages to consumers. Exterior signage attracts passing trade, while signage inside the retail environment is used for both navigational and promotional purposes. The tent card at the checkout, the (invariably) red and white posters and banners that trumpet 'SALE', the branded fascia running the width of the store front – each form of signage has a distinct role to play.

Contribution to Retail History

As well being informative, shop signage also provides a 'canvas' through which retailers can speak to their customers, promote and differentiate their brand, inside and outside their premises.

Ledger

ORIGINALLY A LEDGER WAS
THE NAME FOR A SERVICE BOOK
KEPT IN ONE PLACE IN A CHURCH
– "THE CURATES SHOULD PROVIDE
A BOOK OF THE BIBLE IN ENGLISH,
OF THE LARGEST VOLUME, TO BE A
LEDGER IN THE SAME CHURCH FOR THE
PARISHIONERS TO READ ON."

The actual system of reconciling balances was invented by the famous and successful 15th century Italian banking family: the Medici. They developed the double entry system of tracking credits and debits in a ledger. Their Medici currency was once the most used in Europe, and the principles of their ledger system are still in use today – even if many are now computerised.

If you want to total up your financial transactions for the day, week or month, no doubt you will have some kind of ledger to record those 'takings' in. On the page in front of you the debits and credits are shown in different columns and there's a balance when you begin and one when you end. The golden rule is that every debit recorded must have a credit, so that in the grand total when you finish, the debits equal the credits.

Contribution to Retail History

Bookkeeping – or keeping the ledgers – was, and remains, fundamental to a retailer's ability to track and balance goods in against goods out. The resulting financial metrics produce a clear gauge of how well the business is doing and can be used to evaluate the success of business strategies.

Royal Exchange

THE ROYAL EXCHANGE IN LONDON WAS ESTABLISHED IN 1565 BY THOMAS GRESHAM TO SERVE AS A CENTRE FOR FINANCIAL TRADING, AS WELL AS, COMMERCE.

THE ROYAL EXCHANGE WAS A FORERUNNER TO THE MODERN SHOPPING MALL AS GRESHAM HAD THE VISION TO DEDICATE SEVERAL FLOORS OF THE STRUCTURE TO RETAIL USES AND COLLECT RENT FROM TENANTS WHO OCCUPIED THE SPACE.

Thomas Gresham was a wealthy businessman who set out to change the crude financial trading practices that were common in London during the 16th century. Gresham had served as a royal agent for both King Edward VI and Queen Mary and spent time at the bourse in the Belgian city of Antwerp and wanted to bring a similar concept to London. He invested a large portion of his personal wealth to construct a bourse on land provided by the city of London between Cornhill and Threadneedle Street. Queen Elizabeth I officially opened the Royal Exchange in 1571 and the timing could not have been better for several reasons. London's population was expanding rapidly and the nation's ascension as a global power had created newfound wealth among residents who were eager to purchase merchandise from retailers who occupied the upper floors of the Royal Exchange.

In addition, the Royal Exchange brought London's financial trading activities up to the standards of continental Europe at a pivotal moment. The completion of the facility five years prior to the Spanish sacking of Antwerp set London on a course to become the financial capital of Europe.

The original structure stood for nearly 100 years before it was destroyed by fire in 1666. A rebuilt structure that opened three years later was again destroyed by fire in 1838. The third Royal Exchange building, which still stands today, was reopened in 1844. The financial firms left the Royal Exchange in 1939 and it became a purely retail establishment.

Contribution to Retail History

The Royal Exchange is considered by many to be the world's first shopping mall. Founder Thomas Gresham established the principle of combining multiple shopkeepers under a single roof to offer a broad range of merchandise categories to create a compelling retail destination.

In-Store Graphic

THERE ARE EXAMPLES OF SIGNS IN SHOPS AND TRADING HOUSES PRESERVED IN THE RUINS OF POMPEII AND HERCULANEUM — SOME IN PAINTED FORM CASUALLY PAINTED ONTO SHUTTERS AND PANELLING AND OBVIOUSLY TEMPORARY, OTHERS PERMANENTLY CARVED INTO THE SHOP STONEWORK.

These signs suggest that Roman shopkeepers seldom used their names to identify their shop — a butcher, for example, might identify his trade by painting a sheep. This form of identity was a widespread practice in Europe until the 17th century when shopkeepers began to put their names on the shop fascia - thus began the process of brand identity and reputation. Today store communications fall into three categories: Information (way finding, price, weight, provenance, product content and so forth); Promotion (sale, special offer, and more) and Emotional and Positional. The graphics in this latter category may not be product-specific, but might be images of contented cows inferring ethical farming, or others conveying images of traditional craftsmanship. But in all cases, graphics serve to promote a brand's position and reputation.

"Brand is but Trust spelt differently" and in the modern shopping context, whether it is digital on the shop screen, or in the physical shopping space, store communications in whatever form, are increasing. But they are also subject to scrutiny for accuracy and truthfulness and as such, play a critical role in demonstrating the brand's integrity.

GRAPHIC SIGNAGE, AS A FORM OF STORE TO CUSTOMER COMMUNICATION, HAS EXISTED FOR AS LONG AS THERE HAVE BEEN SHOPS.

Contribution to Retail History

Graphic signage in stores helps to create the tonal atmosphere that reflects the store's positioning. Used to inform or promote, their distinctive designs brought new rewards for the retailers.

4

1700 to 1900

MASS
PRODUCTION

Department Store

DEPARTMENT STORES, AS THE NAME SUGGESTS, OFFER SHOPPERS A BROAD ASSORTMENT OF MERCHANDISE ARRANGED IN DEPARTMENTS TO SATISFY A WIDE RANGE OF WANTS AND NEEDS.

THE EARLIEST DEPARTMENT STORES APPEALED TO AFFLUENT SHOPPERS OR THOSE WHO ASPIRED TO OWN HIGH-QUALITY MERCHANDISE AND BEGAN TO SURFACE ON MULTIPLE CONTINENTS IN THE EARLY TO MID-1800S. THE DEPARTMENT STORE CONCEPT REMAINS HIGHLY RELEVANT TO SHOPPERS, BUT MODERN OPERATORS ARE LESS DISCRIMINATING AND OFFER FORMATS AND PRODUCT ASSORTMENTS THAT APPEAL TO A BROAD RANGE OF INCOME LEVELS.

As with many retail innovations, the origins of the department store are difficult to isolate to a particular individual or retailer and the earliest versions of department stores bore little resemblance to their modern counterparts. However, what is clear is that the concept of a retail store offering multiple classifications of merchandise gained momentum in the early to mid-1800s.

Charles Henry Harrod established his first retail business in London 1824. Austin's was established as a department store in Northern Ireland in 1830 and David Jones opened a department store in Australia in 1838. Emerson Muschamp Bainbridge and William Alder Dunn opened a department store in England in 1849 and in 1851, the Buckley & Nunn department store opened in Melbourne, Australia. In 1852, Aristide Boucicaut opened the Le Bon Marché in Paris and six years later in 1958 the first R.H. Macy & Co. store opened in New York.

These retailers brought a different perspective to the concept of department store, but each sought to benefit from the escalating standard of living that had resulted from the Industrial Revolution. As disposable incomes for Europeans and Americans increased, department store operators were there to provide a new type of shopping experience and to satisfy shoppers' desire for consumer goods.

The golden age of the traditional department store and its role in society began to fade in the 1960s with the advent of suburban shopping malls and discount department stores. The latter introduced a new type of value proposition to price sensitive mass market shoppers who were willing to accept reduced service levels and a more austere store experience in exchange for lower prices.

The concept of the department store remains as relevant as ever, however retailers have to continue to refine product assortments and pursue ever narrower segments of the marketplace based on shopper demographics.

www.retail100objects.com

Contribution to Retail History

The introduction of department stores in England, France and the United States in the early to mid-1800s marked the beginning of an important chapter in the history of retailing. Department stores became iconic symbols of prosperity and were the dominant form of retailing for more than a century. The concept of the department store remains as highly relevant today as when it emerged to satisfy newfound affluence spawned by the Industrial Revolution. Department stores gave rise to discount stores and also influenced the development of enclosed malls as retail developers took note of the powerful appeal that resulted from combining multiple departments of merchandise in a single destination.

Pocket Balance

A POCKET BALANCE – ALSO KNOWN AS A SPRING SCALE – IS SIMPLY A SPRING FIXED AT ONE END WITH A HOOK TO WHICH AN OBJECT CAN BE ATTACHED AT THE OTHER.

THE OBJECT TO BE WEIGHED IS HUNG FROM THE HOOK AND THE FORCE THAT THIS WEIGHT EXERTS ON THE SPRING IS PROPORTIONAL TO THE DISTANCE THAT SPRING IS EXTENDED – AN ESTABLISHED SCIENTIFIC PRINCIPLE KNOWN AS HOOKE'S LAW. THE SCALE MARKINGS ON THE SPRING BALANCE IDENTIFY THE WEIGHT ACCORDINGLY.

The pocket balance was first created in 1770 by Richard Salter in the UK. From the late 18th century onwards these little scales were widely used in markets, grocers and farm shops – wherever people needed to be able to verify the weight of goods to be purchased in order to calculate the correct pricing. Portable, quick and simple to use, the pocket balance was ideal for weighing goods where pinpoint accuracy was not required, for example, sacks of potatoes or meat carcasses.

The underlying principles of the spring balance were later incorporated into the spring scale weighing system widely used by retailers. In this case, the items are placed on a tray underneath the spring mechanism and the pressure exerted (expressed as weight) is shown by the position of pointer on the numbered dial.

Contribution to Retail History

The portable spring scale was the first major development in weighing scales that didn't rely on the use of counterweights. Their portability enabled goods to be weighed anywhere, not only in shops or other fixed locations. Spring scales are still in use today because they are cheap to make and easy to use, although in the retail environment, more accurate digital scales have replaced them.

Galaries du Bois

SHOPPING IN PARIS IS JUST AS IMPORTANT AS EATING, WALKING, AND VISITING MUSEUMS, AND THE PRE-20TH CENTURY SHOPPING MALLS OF PARIS ARE STILL AN ATTRACTION FOR TOURISTS TODAY.

THE MALLS HAVE LONG IRON STRUCTURED GLASS ROOFS, AND ORIGINAL FEATURES SUCH AS MARBLE AND BLACK AND WHITE TILED FLOORS. THEY HOUSE RESTAURANTS, SHOPS AND BOUTIQUES.

The passages were built in the style of a 'souk' – a covered area in which to shop, browse and meet friends. The Galeries du Bois au Palais-Royal was built in 1786 and housed 120 luxury boutiques; after shopping there you could pop in to the central gardens that housed the Palais Royal. The Galeries du Bois became the prototype for the other passages of Paris that followed.

The upper classes loved these malls. They could shop and meet, away from noise, smells, weather and 'unsightly riff-raff'. Famous writers and other notables visited them. Balzac and Zola wrote about them in their books.

By 1850 Paris had 150 passages, but today just 30 remain. Department stores such as Bon Marché, which opened in 1852, began to replace them.

Contribution to Retail History

The Galeries du Bois form another link in the chain of the history of public shopping 'centres', which stretches back to the forums of Ancient Rome. The 18th century Parisian 'galleries' share many features with today's modern malls – a covered, pleasant retail environment where shopping is a social pastime, as well as, a commercial activity.

Chain Store

THE ORIGINS OF MODERN CHAIN STORE RETAILING DATE BACK SEVERAL MILLENNIA TO ANCIENT CHINA. MERCHANTS IN CHINA AND LATER JAPAN RECOGNISED THERE WERE ADVANTAGES TO CENTRALISED MANAGEMENT AND SELLING THROUGH MULTIPLE DISTRIBUTION POINTS WHICH TODAY SERVE AS THE DEFINING CHARACTERISTICS OF CHAIN STORE RETAILING.

CHAIN STORES EMERGED IN NORTH AMERICA IN THE 1700S WHEN THE HUDSON'S BAY COMPANY CREATED A NETWORK OF BRANDED TRADING POSTS.

However, it wasn't until the end of the 19th century that the chain store approach to retail gained momentum in Europe and the United States. The era of chain store expansion began in earnest in the early 20th century as retailers recognised the profit potential associated with leveraging a variety of fixed and variable costs across an expanding base of stores whereby the sales volume generated by each additional location produced incremental profits. The superiority of the chain store business model became evident following the Second World War when global consumption surged for all manner of consumer goods. This set off an unprecedented wave of chain store expansion across all types of merchandise classifications.

Definitions on the number of units that constitute a chain may vary, but there is no disputing the chain store's impact on retailing. Chain stores led a dramatic restructuring of the retail industry during the past 100 years and today many of the world's largest corporations are chain store operations.

Contribution to Retail History

The chain store method of retailing brought about arguably the greatest structural change the industry has seen during the past 100 years. The retail industry today is dominated by those who operate chain stores to effectively serve consumers' wants and needs in a profitable manner.

www.retail100objects.com

Chalkboard

THE USE OF THE CHALKBOARD (ALSO KNOWN AS BLACKBOARD) INITIALLY FOUND FAVOUR AS A TEACHING AID.

ITS FIRST USE IN SCHOOL IS ATTRIBUTED TO JAMES PILLANS, HEADMASTER OF THE OLD HIGH SCHOOL IN EDINBURGH, WHO IS SAID TO HAVE INTRODUCED THE USE OF COLOURED CHALKS ON BLACKBOARDS TO TEACH HIS GEOGRAPHY LESSONS.

In 1801, George Baron, an English mathematician who was teaching at West Point Military Academy, became the first instructor in America to deploy the chalkboard in class.

The popularity of the chalkboard spread rapidly; not only did it enable teachers to communicate in writing with a whole class, it cut down on the use of costly paper, ink and pencils. Chalkboards soon became equally important in business organisations for presentations and brain storming new concepts among several people at once.

Not surprisingly, the chalkboard caught on quickly amongst retailers, offering a highly adaptable approach to signage. Easily updated, with clear 'black on white' messaging, they were cheap and quick to use. Today, traditional chalks have been joined by 'liquid' and 'digital' chalks, but the essential quality of the chalkboard itself remains unchanged.

Contribution to Retail History

Quickly changed and updateable, blackboards continue to be used by market traders, retailers and restaurateurs around the world. They are particularly popular for promoting 'artisan' style products in specialist shops because of their ability to convey a sense of authenticity and a 'hand crafted' feel. Their 'here today, gone tomorrow' adaptability makes them a cost-effective option for seasonal and promotional messaging.

Gas Light

The notion of burning various fuels to produce artificial light is as old as fire itself. However, open flames were impractical and the light they generated was dim at best. Lanterns that burned liquid fuels were an upgrade in terms of safety and light quality, but it wasn't until gas was harnessed as a power source that lighting made its most meaningful advance.

The burning of combustible gasses as a means to produce artificial light was first recognised by William Murdoch, an employee of the Soho Foundry steam engine works in Birmingham, England. In 1790, Murdoch used goal gas to light his home and later the main building of the foundry where he worked.

Urban areas throughout England soon recognised the benefits of using gas to light streets and by the first quarter of the 19th century major cities and towns throughout Europe were reliant on gas street lamps. The expense of gas lighting limited its use to cities, business and wealthy homeowners until later in the 19th century.

Around that time the efficiency of gas lighting would make a major step forward with the introduction of a device known as a 'mantle' that allowed the burning gas to create a brighter light. The device also allowed gas lighting to remain relevant longer than it might have otherwise and to fend off competition from newly emerging electrical lighting technology, which was unproven and thought to be unsafe at the time.

The usage of gas lighting remained common in developed nations during the early part of the 20th century, but it gradually succumbed to the more efficient, brighter and safer electrical lighting. Today, gas lighting serves primarily as an ornamental function to evoke images of a bygone era.

Gas was a popular and economical method of lighting common throughout the 19th century. Retailers relied on gas lighting to illuminate walkways, store fronts and building interiors before the advent of electricity made doing so simpler, safer and brighter.

Contribution to Retail History

Gas lighting and the illumination it provided to public space changed urban lifestyles and consequently the retail industry. Streetlights made previously dark roadways and walkways safe and inviting during evening hours. Pedestrians and operators of carriages and later vehicles gained the freedom to engage in activities such as shopping that had previously been reserved for daylight hours. Retailers were beneficiaries of gas lighting because they could extend operating hours to accommodate more customers and shift administrative tasks to non-operating hours.

Price Tag

PRICE TAGS SIMPLIFY THE PROCESS OF SHOPPING BY INSTANTLY CONVEYING THE COST OF MERCHANDISE TO PROSPECTIVE BUYERS WHO ARE THEN BETTER ABLE TO MAKE A PURCHASE DECISION.

PRICE TAGS CAN TAKE MANY FORMS BUT ALL REPRESENT A FIXED, RATHER THAN NEGOTIABLE PRICE, FOR MERCHANDISE AND SIMPLIFY RETAIL OPERATIONS BY ALLOWING CENTRALISED DECISION-MAKING. PRICE TAGS ARE AN ESSENTIAL ELEMENT OF THE RETAIL EXPERIENCE.

The humble price tag, taken for granted by shoppers in modern retail outlets, was a major development in the evolution of retail. Thought by many to have come into vogue around the mid-19th century, the price tag is another innovation credited to the early operators of department stores. The actual origin is difficult to isolate, but extensive use of price tags was known to exist at the Le Bon Marché department store founded by Aristide Boucicaut in 1852.

The concept of openly displaying merchandise and clearly communicating the cost of goods via tags was a novel idea at the time. It quickly gained acceptance with other retailers who recognised that shoppers found the practice desirable and also understood the important business implications.

Price tags take many forms today and thanks to the advent of the barcode and shelf edge pricing, most fast moving consumer goods no longer bear individual prices. Barcodes eliminated the need for price

tags on some products, but their usage remains widespread on products such as apparel, footwear, accessories and hard line categories of goods. These products will typically have some form of a price tag as well as a barcode, even though in some instances a secondary pricing sign on a display will be used to override the price printed on the tag.

Price tags have gone digital as well with electronic shelf labels, or ESLs, employed by some retailers. ESLs offer a new approach to ensure accuracy and optimise margins by employing dynamic pricing strategies based on shifting demand and competitive circumstances.

Contribution to Retail History

The price tag represented a major advancement in price transparency. Shoppers were able to instantly understand the cost of an item and make a purchase decision without the aid of a retail employee. Knowledge of a product's price encouraged sales and offered a myriad of business benefits to retailers, the most significant of which was the ability to manage profitability by understanding the margin contribution of different products and categories. Price tags were a key enabler of self-service shopping and led to the introduction of mark downs, both as a means to clear slow-moving goods and as a mechanism to showcase savings from the anchoring price.

Doorbell

IN THE 19TH CENTURY, STORE DOORBELLS WERE NOT ELECTRIC. TYPICALLY MADE OF SOLID BRASS, THE BELL WAS ATTACHED TO AN ARM THAT WAS IN TURN MOUNTED ON A SPRING ON THE INSIDE OF THE DOOR. THUS, AS SOON AS THE DOOR OPENED, THE BELL SOUNDED, ALERTING THE RETAILER TO THE ARRIVAL (OR DEPARTURE) OF A CUSTOMER.

THIS SIMPLE DEVICE WAS INVALUABLE FOR BUSY STOREKEEPERS WHO DID NOT HAVE THE RESOURCES TO MAINTAIN A MEMBER OF STAFF ON THE SHOP FLOOR THROUGHOUT EVERY OPENING HOUR. OFTEN, MUCH OF THEIR TIME WAS SPENT 'OUT BACK' TAKING DELIVERY OF GOODS, OR DOING BOOK-KEEPING.

The first bell that could be triggered by an electric wire connected to a bell was invented by Joseph Henry around 1831. Then in 1881, Edwin Swan of Indiana patented an electric doorbell called 'the illuminated electric push button'. Today, smaller shops still make use of the bell system to herald the entry of a customer. The classic brass bell has been replaced by a plethora of chime choices, two-tone rings, buzzes, bleeps and more.

The doorbell continues to play a key role in a reversed retail situation, that of door-to-door selling. From the earliest days of trading when peddlers would travel from place to place selling their wares, the knock at the door – or ringing of the bell in the street – would alert the prospective customer to the arrival of goods for sale.

Contribution to Retail History

From medieval traders to the spring bell at the back of the shopkeeper's door, from Avon Cosmetics' memorable 'Ding Dong – Avon Calling' marketing campaign to a child's reaction to the unmistakable sound of an ice cream van's chime, the ringing of a bell retains its association as the herald of a buying opportunity.

Display Window

WHEN IN THE 1840S ADVANCES IN GLASS PRODUCTION ENABLED LARGE PANES OF GLASS TO BE USED IN SHOP FRONTS, THE DEPARTMENT STORES BEGAN TO TAKE THE CONCEPT OF WINDOW DISPLAYS TO A NEW LEVEL.

Retailers quickly recognised that their windows were a leveragable resource and the growth of the department store in the early 20th century saw window dressing become a serious business. Rival stores used their windows as three-dimensional advertising hoardings, producing incredibly theatrical and flamboyant displays to outplay their competitors in luring customers across their threshold.

Today, professional window dressers (or merchandisers) and even sometimes well-known artists, are commissioned to combine fashion, design and marketing to create seasonal or otherwise themed temporary 'art installations'. Colour, props, lighting, moving parts and film footage, and sometimes even real people, are used to highlight and differentiate the store's offering. In a retail world where most department stores are selling the same ranges and products, the display window has a vital role to play in giving a retail brand name a distinctive image and set of associations.

DISPLAY WINDOWS HAVE ALWAYS BEEN USED TO TEMPT CUSTOMERS INTO STORES. THE FIRST SHOPKEEPERS USED OSTENTATIOUS SIGNS WITH THEIR NAMES OVER THEIR DOORS, AND PLACED THEIR PRODUCTS PROUDLY IN THE WINDOWS OF THEIR SHOPS TO ATTRACT THE ATTENTION OF PASSING TRADE.

Contribution to Retail History

Early 19th century shop windows tended to be small, crowded spaces with goods piled high, seldom displayed to their best advantage. The arrival of plate glass transformed them into great showcases that still turn a shopping thoroughfare into a battleground across which retailers fight to capture the elusive attention of passing trade and define the store proposition.

Sewing Machine

UP UNTIL THE EARLY 19TH CENTURY, MOST WORKING-CLASS WOMEN MADE THE CLOTHES FOR THEIR FAMILIES BY HAND. WEALTHIER FAMILIES EMPLOYED SEAMSTRESSES AND TAILORS TO DO THE SAME.

FOLLOWING SEVERAL YEARS OF ATTEMPTS THE DEVELOPMENT OF A SEWING MACHINE (MADE BY A NUMBER OF INVENTORS, MOST OF WHOM COULD LAY CLAIM TO HAVING INFLUENCED THE VERSION THAT EVENTUALLY SUCCEEDED), ISAAC SINGER BUILT THE FIRST COMMERCIALLY VIABLE MACHINE IN 1850.

Mass production of these machines for household and industrial application quickly followed and the sewing machine became the first durable, technologically complex household appliance in America (and in Britain soon after). Industrial use of sewing machines moved clothing production away from the housewives and seamstresses and into large-scale factories. This resulted in a decrease in the amount of time clothing production took, which in turn caused prices for clothing to drop.

For many existing garment manufacturers, the installation of sewing machines greatly reduced the manpower they needed to employ, and numbers of employees in some clothing factories dropped sharply. But this was the time of the Industrial Revolution and many of the workers found new employment in other factories. A further swelling of the potential workforce was seen in those women who had previously been kept busy hand sewing at home now being liberated to go out to work, thus increasing the family income. Rising income meant families could afford to buy more ready-made garments, thus creating more demand.

The sewing machine's effects on the clothing industry resulted in major changes for other industries as well. Cotton production increases in order to meet the demands of the new clothing factories, with associated impacts on foreign trade and development. Machine production democratised fashion, transforming the social meaning of clothing by making stylish garments available to almost everyone.

Contribution to Retail History

The sewing machine saw the birth of the clothing manufacturing and retail industry as we know it today, creating a supply and demand for ready-made garments. In response, retailers specialising in garment sales sprang up in towns and cities all over the world. The move away from bespoke, handmade items to mass production was one of the major characteristics of the industrialised era.

EARLY CIVILISATIONS USED ICE CAVES, SNOW AND COLD STREAMS TO KEEP FOODSTUFFS COLD. THE CHINESE CUT AND STORED ICE IN 1,000 BC AND AROUND 500 BC, THE EGYPTIANS AND INDIANS WOULD PUT WATER OUT IN EARTHENWARE POTS TO CHILL OVERNIGHT.

Refrigeration

IN THE EARLY 18TH CENTURY, 'ICE HOUSES' BEGAN TO BE CREATED; THESE WERE STORES FOR LARGE BLOCKS OF ICE (HARVESTED FROM FROZEN LAKES), WHICH WERE THEN PACKED TOGETHER WITH SAWDUST OR FLANNEL AND SALT.

Attempts at refrigerated transport for the shipping of perishable goods began in the mid-18th century. The first refrigerated railroad car was introduced by the Northern Railroad (New York) in 1851. Known as the 'icebox on wheels' the fact that it only functioned in cold weather rather limited its value.

However, within the food production industries, refrigeration was gaining traction. By the 1880s, breweries were the largest users of commercial refrigeration units and by 1900, the meat packing houses of Chicago had ammonia style commercial fridges. By the start of the First World War refrigeration in packing plants in the US was widespread.

By the middle of the 20th century, the technology for refrigerated vehicles had progressed and throughout the developed world perishable goods were being shipped by road, rail and air, to stores thousands of miles from where the produce had originated.

Contribution to Retail History

Refrigeration radically changed the capabilities and potential of every stage of the supply chain. Producers could now pack and process fresh food and create new product ranges; distributors were able to transport those food products all over the globe, knowing they would still be fresh (or frozen) on arrival. With the installation of chiller and frozen food cabinets, supermarkets were able to significantly innovate and expand the range and volume of goods they sold, and a new strand of retailing emerged – the frozen food store. For the customer, home fridges and freezers revolutionised their shopping habits; the move towards the large volume, weekly food shop began, as there was no longer the need to buy perishable goods on a daily basis.

Elevator

LIFT AND PULLEY SYSTEMS WERE IN USE FROM ANCIENT TIMES BUT IT TOOK A ROYAL COMMISSION FROM LOUIS XV OF FRANCE (IN THE 17TH CENTURY) WHO WANTED A COUNTERWEIGHT LIFT FOR HIS WIFE, BEFORE PASSENGER ELEVATORS (LIFTS) BEGAN TO TAKE SHAPE.

HOWEVER, PEOPLE REMAINED MISTRUSTFUL OF THE CONCEPT AND IT WAS ONLY WHEN ELISHA GRAVES OTIS INVENTED – AND PUBLICLY DEMONSTRATED – THE FIRST SAFETY BRAKE FOR ELEVATORS, THAT THE POTENTIAL FOR TAKING BUILDINGS HIGHER THAN A PERSON COULD COMFORTABLY CLIMB REALLY TOOK OFF.

The very first commercial installation undertaken by Otis was in 1857, at a five-storey department store in New York City. His achievement was widely acclaimed and today's familiar high-rise cityscapes began to emerge rapidly, each reaching higher than the last. The first electric elevator was built by Werner von Siemens in 1880 in Germany.

Businesses, hotels, retail outlets and others all began to maximise their floorspace by building upwards. In 1946, the JL Hudson department store on Woodward Avenue in Detroit, Michigan, was completed. It had 33 levels and remained the tallest department store in the world until the 1960s.

Working alongside escalators, elevators transport shoppers from floor to floor, but they fulfill a broader function in that they are also vital for the transportation of goods between floors. Further back in the retail supply chain, elevators and the principles of platforms on pulleys are used throughout manufacturing and production plants and distribution centres.

The award-winning Burj Khalifa tower building in Dubai emphasises just how essential a modern day elevator is for trade and business to flourish. When construction began in 2004, its planners proclaimed it would house the 'largest shopping mall in the world'. Without elevators, its 160 floors would be of little appeal to even the hardiest shopper.

Contribution to Retail History

The multi-floored department stores, shopping centres and outlets that we shop in today could not exist were it not for their elevators. They keep customers moving quickly, reliably and efficiently through the shopping environment, and speed the distribution of stock. Constantly being refined, they have become ever faster and smoother.

Catalogue

IN 1872, AARON MONTGOMERY, WARD OF CHICAGO, PRODUCED THE FIRST MAIL-ORDER CATALOGUE FOR HIS MONTGOMERY WARD MAIL ORDER BUSINESS, AIMED AT FARMERS IN THE MIDWEST WHO WERE SUSPICIOUS OF MERCHANTS.

BY SELLING DIRECT TO THE CUSTOMER, WARD COULD AVOID HIS GOODS HAVING THE RETAILER'S MARK UP APPLIED, THEREBY REDUCING THE COST TO THOSE CUSTOMERS.

The first catalogue was a single sheet of paper with a price list, just 8 by 12 inches, showing what was for sale and how to go about ordering it. Within 20 years, Ward's original single page list of products had grown into a 540-page illustrated book and he was by then, selling over 20,000 items. From 1921 to 1931 he even sold prefabricated kit houses by mail order. These were called 'Wardway Homes'.

Others all over the world began to sell via mail order too. The T Eaton Co. Limited of Toronto, produced its first 34-page catalogue in 1884. By 1920 it had mail order warehouses in Winnipeg, Toronto and Moncton. It opened its first catalogue office in Oakville in 1916 and others followed. Richard Warren Sears published the first Sears catalogue in 1888. It captured the catalogue industry in the USA and became a byword for catalogue shopping.

In the UK, Sir John Moores set up his 'Littlewoods Mail Order Store'. The first catalogue was published in May 1932 with 168 pages and the motto: "We hoist our Flag in the Port of Supply and right away we sail to the Ports of Demand – the Homes of The People". Moores learned from the examples of his American contemporaries (Montgomery Ward, Sears and Roebuck) and by 1936 the Littlewoods catalogue annual turnover had reached £4 million.

Contribution to Retail History

The development of mail order shopping by the likes of Sears democratised retail, opening up the availability of consumer goods to huge swathes of the population worldwide. Today catalogues can be seen as the precursor to e-commerce, as the principles of internet shopping follow similar lines.

www.retail100objects.com

Denim

THE NAME DENIM IS A SHORT FORM OF 'SERGE DE NÎMES' BECAUSE THIS FORM OF TWILLED COTTON ORIGINATED FROM NÎMES IN FRANCE. DENIM WAS USED IN EUROPE FROM AT LEAST THE END OF THE 17TH CENTURY, BUT ITS POPULARITY ESCALATED RAPIDLY IN THE USA DURING THE 1870S GOLD RUSH.

AMERICAN GOLD MINERS NEEDED DURABLE CLOTHING. TO MEET THIS DEMAND, A MAN CALLED LEOB (LATER LEVI) STRAUSS CREATED A STRONG STYLE OF WORKERS' TROUSERS AND OVERALLS, INCORPORATING COPPER RIVETS ON THE MAIN STRESS POINTS.

These items were quickly adopted by Californian miners and became their wardrobe staple. Originally made from uncomfortable hemp, Strauss switched to using denim, and jeans were born.

In the 1940s, Western films became popular and the appearance of cowboys in jeans on screen prompted a demand for the garment amongst American consumers – creating arguably the first iconic retail clothing item with appeal to a broad audience. Fewer jeans were produced during the Second World War, but the sight of American soldiers wearing them off duty continued to fuel the interest in denim, both in the United States and abroad.

In the 1950s, denim became less a symbol of national pride and more one of teenage rebellion against conformity, as represented by films such as 'Rebel Without a Cause'. Wearers were often refused admission to cinemas, restaurants and other establishments. But recognition of the versatility and comfort of jeans grew and in the 1960s, they became more acceptable (and also individualised as the trend for customising them with embroidery and patches took hold during that era). By the 1970s, denim was firmly established as being fashionable and ubiquitous – no small achievement. The 1980s saw the advent of 'designer jeans' and denim took to the catwalks; today almost every label has its own denim line.

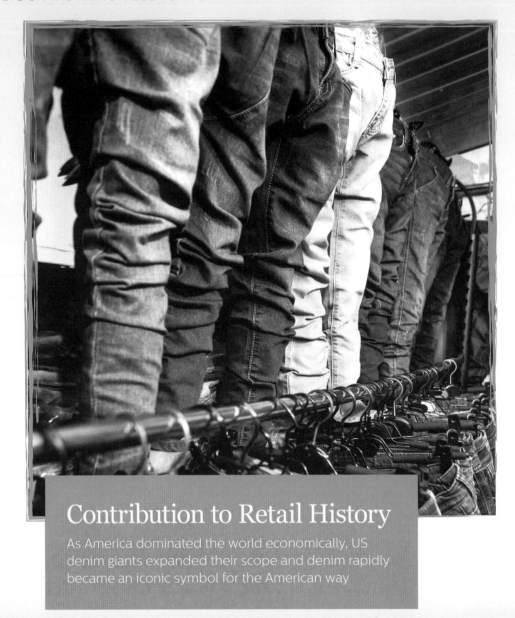

Contribution to Retail History

As America dominated the world economically, US denim giants expanded their scope and denim rapidly became an iconic symbol for the American way

PNEUMATIC TUBE TRANSPORT, OR PTT, ALLOWS THE USERS TO PUT SOLID OBJECTS INTO A NETWORK OF TUBES FOR TRANSPORTATION ALONG THOSE TUBES BY COMPRESSED AIR OR BY PARTIAL VACUUM.

Pneumatic Tube Transport System

THESE TUBES BECAME POPULAR WITH RETAILERS IN THE LATE 19TH AND EARLY 20TH CENTURY, WHO USED THEM TO SEND MESSAGES OR MONEY OVER SHORT DISTANCES WITHIN THEIR STORES, OR IN RARE INSTANCES, ACROSS THE CITY.

Early pneumatic post or mail systems were invented by the Scottish engineer William Murdoch, in the 19th century. The London Pneumatic Despatch Companies postal systems were said to be powerful enough to transport humans during trial runs (but they never actually put a person inside).

In July 1875 D. Brown patented a pneumatic tube system called the 'Cash Carrier'. Designed for in-store use, the cash carrier transported cash and coins through large department stores and was used to great effect for many decades. One of the earliest retail adopters of the PTT system was Wanamaker's department store in Philadelphia, which installed the system in 1880, just a year after installing electric lighting.

Its use as a mail and message carrier was also effective. For nearly sixty years (1897 to 1953), the New York City Post Office used PTT (operated by the Tubular Dispatch Company) to distribute mail. In 1914 almost a third of New York City's first class mail was distributed via this method.

While email has superseded the use of pneumatic tubes for delivering messages, they are still widely used by banks, hospitals, factories and larger department stores for transporting small items and money. For retailers, the tubes offer a way to move cash from the checkout to the back office, and send change back to the cashiers.

Contribution to Retail History

Transporting cash and till receipts via the PTT had a big impact on the safety and efficiency of money handling within the retail environment. Cashiers finishing a shift could send their takings and corresponding till roll direct to the accounting office, enabling the office to differentiate and account for takings across cashiers and shifts. A much safer way of transporting cash, it reduced theft and store 'shrinkage' by removing the risk of takings being intercepted on the journey from till to accounts and ensured the tills never held too much money at any one time. As a genius invention that customers could see being put to work, the PTT system also created a bit of 'theatre' in the store.

Soda Fountain

ALTHOUGH ITS ORIGINS LIE IN EUROPE, THE SODA FOUNTAIN ACHIEVED ITS GREATEST SUCCESS IN THE USA. THROUGHOUT THE 20TH CENTURY THEY WERE TO BE FOUND IN AMERICAN PHARMACIES, ICE CREAM PARLOURS, SWEET SHOPS, DEPARTMENT STORES, MILK BARS AND TRAIN STATIONS. THEY REACHED THE HEIGHT OF THEIR SALES IN THE 1940s AND 1950s.

BETWEEN 1810 AND 1903, A SERIES OF US PATENTS WERE ISSUED FOR THE PRODUCTION AND DISTRIBUTION OF IMITATION MINERAL AND SODA FOUNTAINS. THESE DEVELOPMENTS LED, IN THE EARLY 20TH CENTURY, TO PHARMACIES AND OTHER SHOPS SELLING SODA DRINKS, ADDING THE SYRUP BY HAND TO CREATE FLAVOURED CARBONATED WATER. AT FIRST, THE FLAVOURING WAS ADDED TO MASK THE TASTE OF THE MEDICINAL MINERAL WATER, BUT IT QUICKLY BECAME AN END PRODUCT IN ITSELF.

By 1875, there was a soda fountain in almost every city across America and they were entrenched in American culture. Over the ensuing decades, the soda fountain became an ever more popular gathering place. The name became extended to mean both the dispensing equipment and the outlet in which sodas were sold. During Prohibition in the 1920s (when the sale of alcohol was banned), the soda fountain offered an alternative to the speakeasy. Later, as American consumers struggled through the Great Depression of the 1930s, the soda fountains provided an affordable luxury.

An early example of the benefits of combining the sale of refreshments within the retail environment, the soda fountain generated additional footfall to the stores in which they were situated. These customers lingered longer in the store, creating a captive audience that was more likely to purchase other goods before leaving.

By the 1960s, the popularity of soda fountains was declining, due to competition from fast food outlets, bottled soft drinks and the rise in diners and restaurants.

Contribution to Retail History

The soda fountain was a cultural and social phenomenon. Attracting people to the stores and generating additional sales when they were there, the soda fountain made first the drugstore, then the convenience store, a place for retail and social commerce.

THE GALLERIA VITTORIO EMANUELE II IS THE OLDEST SHOPPING MALL IN ITALY, HOUSED IN A FOUR STOREY BUILDING IN MILAN.

Galleria Vittorio Emanuele II

DESIGNED IN 1861, AND BUILT BETWEEN 1865 AND 1877, THE GALLERIA IS NAMED AFTER VITTORIO EMANUELE II, THE FIRST KING OF THE KINGDOM OF ITALY. IT'S BEEN NICKNAMED 'MILAN'S DRAWING ROOM'.

The roof is a magnificent glass and cast iron octagon, covering the street below, and it was the prototype for today's modern glazed enclosed shopping malls, many of which are also called Galleria. Today, the shops sell luxury goods, haute couture, jewellery, books and paintings, and it is home to many bars, cafes and restaurants too.

In 2012 after 20 years of trading, McDonald's was not allowed to renew its tenancy there, so it sued the City of Milan for $24 million in damages, which represented $6 million a year in sales. A Prada store has replaced it.

Contribution to Retail History

First introduced in Paris at the end of the 18th century, the galleria was the immediate forerunner of the department store. Galleria Emanuele brought this format to its apogee. Important as an early example of the use of retail/hospitality as a method of town planning, the Galleria Emanuele was designed to fill an urban space that would link the high art of the Opera House with the high church of the Duomo.

Unlike most preceding galleria, Emanuele is multi-storey and its architectural concept foretells the design of the grander department stores which blossomed in the fourth quarter of the 19th century, and the modern shopping centres which followed in the 20th.

Retail Advertising

RETAIL ADVERTISING CONSISTS OF MARKETING COMMUNICATIONS DESIGNED TO ESTABLISH THE RETAILER'S IMAGE, SHOWCASE PRODUCT ASSORTMENTS AND PRICE PROMOTIONS AND INFORM SHOPPERS OF STORE LOCATIONS.

SOME RETAIL ADVERTISING FOCUSES ON CHARITABLE EFFORTS WHICH HELPS CULTIVATE A DESIRED IMAGE. RETAILERS USE A WIDE RANGE OF PRINT, ELECTRONIC, OUT-OF-HOME AND DIGITAL OPTIONS FOR ADVERTISING.

The origins of retail advertising can be traced to 17th century Europe. The continent was the centre of global trade and that gave merchants access to an expanded and unfamiliar range of goods. To promote awareness and encourage consumption of their offerings, merchants turned to posters, hand bills and later, newspapers.

Newspapers and other print media dominated retail advertising for centuries and continued to do so even after the introduction of radio and television gave newly emerging chain retailers powerful new ways to reach a mass market.

As consumption exploded following the Second World War so did retail advertising, although it remained highly reliant on print vehicles.

Upscale retailers relied on glossy fashion and lifestyle magazines that appealed to affluent individuals to hone their image as a destination for up market goods. Meanwhile, retailers oriented toward the mass market fed shoppers a steady diet of weekly advertising circulars distributed via direct mail or inserted into the Sunday newspaper that featured promotional prices on key items. The frequency of price-oriented ads helped retailers generate customer traffic to their stores and gave branded suppliers a vehicle to generate awareness and to trial new products that were introduced with increased regularity.

As retailers grew increasingly large, many recognised their sizable base of shoppers was an attractive audience for advertisers and a wide range of in-store communication opportunities were created. The store became an advertising medium unto itself and retailers placed messaging on floor and in shopping carts and hung promotional signs from shelves and ceilings. Some retailers created their own in-store radio and television networks.

Retailers left no stone unturned when it came to communicating with shoppers and this practice has extended to the Internet. Increasingly effective and measurable forms of digital advertising are comprising an ever larger percentage of retailers' ad budgets. That trend will continue as shoppers consume more information from digital sources.

Contribution to Retail History

Retail advertising created some of the largest, most successful and iconic brands in business and contributed to the overall growth of the advertising industry during the past century. Shoppers rely on retail advertising to make informed purchase decisions about where to shop and what to buy.

Telephone

TWO INVENTORS, ELISHA GRAY AND ALEXANDER GRAHAM BELL, CAME UP WITH AN ELECTRICAL DEVICE THAT COULD TRANSMIT SPEECH DOWN WIRES. THEY APPARENTLY GOT TO THE PATENT OFFICE WITHIN HOURS OF EACH OTHER, BUT BELL PIPPED GRAY TO THE POST. BELL WAS AWARDED HIS PATENT IN MARCH 1876.

Elsewhere, also in 1876, a Hungarian engineer, Tivadar Puskas, was inventing the telephone switchboard which ultimately led to the creation of telephone exchanges and then networks. Western Union, who already had telegraph exchanges, began to use them for its telephones in New York City and San Francisco. The benefits of the telephone were quickly seized upon. In 1884, the UK had around 13,000 telephones in use and the Postmaster-General decided to extend their reach. As a result, 'call offices' were installed in shops and other public places.

Towards the end of the 1880s, the growing numbers of installations led to the issuing of telephone numbers. The telephone became indispensable to retailers for communicating with both suppliers and customers, for placing and taking orders. By the middle of the 20th century, the ability for prospective customers to make enquires and order goods led retailers to establish customer service and telesales departments, and to actively promote customer order telephone numbers on their literature and advertising materials.

The early days of the internet relied on dial-up modems using the telephone cabling network, allowing us to take the first steps to e-commerce (online shopping). Wireless and mobile phone technology has taken this retail revolution further. Retailers have been quick to develop mobile apps that can, amongst many other things, incorporate a product catalogue and shopping cart, enabling customers to shop in their store 'virtually', day or night. Prospective customers browsing in store can use their mobiles to take photos of merchandise for reference and share the images with friends via social networks, to seek their opinion prior to making a purchasing decision.

In 1879, Wanamakers (in Philadelphia) became the first department store to install the telephone.

Contribution to Retail History

Whether it's management of the supply chain, customer service or online shopping, the telephone in all its guises has been one of the most fundamental enablers for the retail industry. Call centres around the world have enabled retailers to handle mass inbound telephone ordering (often in response to telesales ads placed across a variety of media) and outbound telesales calling. Today, the advantages of telephone communications can also work against the retailer, as customers are increasingly 'showrooming' — using their mobiles to browse and compare online, before deciding which retail outlet to use for their purchase.

Mannequin

THEY STAND IN THE WINDOW, GAZING PAST US WITH DETACHED HAUTEUR, MODELLING THE LATEST STYLES, TEMPTING US TO GO IN, TRY THOSE CLOTHES ON, AND MAKE A PURCHASE.

THEIR USE ORIGINATED IN THE 15TH CENTURY, WHEN MINIATURE MILLINERS' MANNEQUINS WERE USED TO DEMONSTRATE FASHIONS FOR CUSTOMERS. BUT IT WASN'T UNTIL THE 1880s WHEN PLATE GLASS WINDOWS BEGAN TO BE INSTALLED IN SHOP WINDOWS THAT RETAILERS BEGAN TO PLACE THEM IN THEIR SHOP FRONTS.

These shop front mannequins were made from wax, wood or heavy fabric, and they had iron feet to help them stay upright. Papier-mâché and sawdust were used to give them a more realistic shape, and they often reflected an ideal of beauty. They were also expensive to make.

By the turn of the century, mannequins had given birth to a new industry, 'window trimming'. 'Window trimmers' got more and more artistic. Their mannequins developed facial expressions, glass eyes, and real hair. After the First World War, women's dress changed, and the mannequins changed with them, developing a more realistic, simpler body shape.

Then, in the 1930s came a remarkable development. A New York soap sculptor, Lester Gaba, produced six plaster 'Gaba Girls' for a large department store. They even had names and at a party to unveil them were dressed in jewels and the very best clothes of the time. Gaba took one 'sitting' mannequin (called Cynthia), with him wherever he went. She sat with

her elbow on her knee, cigarette in hand, and travelled by taxi with Lester. She even accompanied him to the opera and sat in his box. Mannequins, it seemed, were the new 'it' girls.

During the Second World War, the mannequins began to look drab, reflecting the clothes rationing of the time. By the late 1940s, they had become happier again and wore smiles. The 1950s and 60s saw mannequins made in new materials, such as fibreglass and plastic. Today, the design potential of mannequins is immense; they can be made to retailers' own specifications in any shape, colour or pose.

Contribution to Retail History

Mannequins were, and remain, central to the art of visual merchandising. Used effectively, their presence improves the overall image of a store (outside and in). They continue to be used in ever more impactful ways by the world's most sophisticated retailers, attracting the eye of the passerby and helping to prompt impulse purchasing.

www.retail100objects.com

Vending Machine

THE FIRST COMMERCIAL COIN OPERATED VENDING MACHINES APPEARED IN LONDON IN THE 1880s, SELLING POSTCARDS AND THEN BOOKS. IN 1888, THE THOMAS ADAMS GUM COMPANY BROUGHT VENDING MACHINES TO THE USA AND IN 1907, THE ROUND CANDY COATED GUMBALL VENDING MACHINES WERE INTRODUCED.

THEY BEGAN TO SPREAD AND BECAME POPULAR, OFFERING MORE GOODS, STAMPS, AND CIGARS TOO. IN THE EARLY 1920s, THE FIRST AUTOMATIC VENDING MACHINES STARTED DISPENSING SODAS INTO CUPS.

In 1926, American William Rower, created the cigarette vending machine and in the 1940s and 1950s, Vendoraltor of California gave us Coca-Cola and Pepsi from machines. Usage and coverage grew, with ever more items being dispensed by the machines. From the 1950s to the 1970s, you could even buy a life insurance policy from vending machines at American airports. Today, the range of goods dispensed by vending machines is extensive – food, drink, tickets, money and fresh farm produce. In some locations, even high value items such as iPads can now be purchased via a vending machine.

In Japan, vending machines have been big business ever since their introduction in the 1950s. Selling everything from hot meals to household products, there is apparently one vending machine per 23 people in Japan. The nation's dense population, limited space and low rates of vandalism make it a vending machine–friendly environment.

Vending machine technology has evolved to incorporate digital signage and touch screen technology and to accept credit cards instead of cash. Many machines are now monitored remotely, enabling optimised inventory, automatic updates on maintenance needs and handling of payment services.

Contribution to Retail History

Vending machines created a new, highly efficient method of retailing, enabling the creation of a distribution point just a hand's reach from a potential customer, whenever they might need it most. Placed in locations of high footfall and often in places where people might find themselves killing time (airports, rail platforms and so on), they encouraged impulse purchasing. Able to vend 24/7, with only restocking/maintenance labour requirements, they offered a cost-effective and secure way to supply consumers on the go with goods that they might not otherwise have considered purchasing.

Cash Register

THE CASH REGISTER WAS NOT INVENTED FOR THE CONVENIENCE OF THE CUSTOMER. IT WAS ORIGINALLY DESIGNED TO STOP EMPLOYEES EMBEZZLING MONEY FROM THEIR EMPLOYERS BY ALERTING THEM TO THE FACT THAT A SALE WAS BEING PROCESSED. TWO AMERICAN INVENTORS, JAMES RITTY AND JOHN BIRCH PATENTED IT IN 1883.

THE FIRST REGISTER MODEL WAS LIKE A MECHANICAL ADDING MACHINE. AS EVERY TRANSACTION WAS ENTERED, THE DRAWER OPENED AND A BELL RANG, TELLING THE MANAGER A SALE HAD TAKEN PLACE. THE MACHINE USED METAL TAPS MARKED WITH DENOMINATIONS TO INDICATE THE AMOUNT OF THE SALE AND HAD A TOTAL ADDER THAT SUMMED UP ALL THE CASH VALUES OF THE KEY PRESSED DURING THE DAY. ADVERTISEMENTS CLAIMED THAT THE REGISTER HAD "THE BELL HEARD ROUND THE WORLD".

Ritty sold his invention to Jacob H. Eckert of Cincinnati, who formed the National Manufacturing Company. Eckert then sold to John H. Patterson, who renamed the company the National Cash Register Company. It was Patterson who adapted the design to add a paper roll to record sales transactions, thus creating a receipt.

It was then down to the employees of the National Cash Register Company to come up with the next advancement. Inventor, Charles Kettering, designed a cash register with an electric motor. By the end of the 19th century and early 20th century, nearly all retailers had installed cash registers.

In the UK, from the 1950s to the 1970s it was the Gross Cash Registers Company that captured a large share of the retail market. In 1971, when the UK changed to decimalisation, the Gross Register was adapted to work in both imperial and decimal coinage. Another brand, Sweda, was also 'decimal ready' and is credited with inventing the first all-mechanical register in the 1930s. It was also the first company to introduce touch-screen based point-of-sale (POS) systems, in 1987.

Today, computerised POS terminals operate across networks. The basic principles remain the same, however, the cash register allows the retailer to keep tabs on what staff and customers are doing and to analyse the information for business, stock control, supply chain and marketing purposes.

Contribution to Retail History

From its initial role as a method by which retailers could verify sales and receipts and reduce fraud, continual innovation has extended the influence of the cash register across broader cash management systems. Equipped with barcode scanning capabilities and now with self-scanning, it is fundamental to the development and management of modern sales data, management information retrieval and storage.

Receipt

RECEIPTS AND PROOF OF PURCHASE HAVE BEEN USED SINCE THE EARLIEST DAYS OF RETAIL TRANSACTION, PROVIDING LEGAL PROOF OF THE TRANSFER OF OWNERSHIP OF GOODS.

HOWEVER, THE MECHANISED GENERATION OF RETAIL RECEIPTS DID NOT OCCUR UNTIL THE LATE 19TH CENTURY. IN 1883, TWO AMERICAN INVENTORS, JAMES RITTY AND JOHN BIRCH, PATENTED THE CASH REGISTER, ENABLING SALES TO BE MONITORED AND DETERRING SALES STAFF FROM PILFERING PROFITS. SUBSEQUENTLY, THE NATIONAL CASH REGISTER COMPANY IMPROVED THE DESIGN OF THE MACHINE BY ADDING A PAPER ROLL TO RECORD SALES TRANSACTIONS. THIS EVOLVED INTO THE RECEIPT AS WE KNOW IT TODAY.

Small and unassuming, the receipt is, in fact, a legal document. It gives consumers a record and proof of their purchase and is the evidence retailers require to return or exchange goods. These days, many receipts include barcodes that allow the transaction to be quickly recognised and validated by the retailer's computer system.

Increasingly, and particularly at supermarket checkouts, till receipts contain far more than just a record of purchases made. Promotional messages can be included, including discount vouchers that are triggered by the nature of the goods the customer has just purchased.

Contribution to Retail History

The receipt not only offers customers assurance and retailers proof of purchase, but the information it carries is relayed to back office computing systems and is used for accounting and reconciliation processes. In some countries, the USA for instance, retailers have to retain information about every receipt so that the tax authorities can verify that no sales have been hidden. Increasingly till receipts are also used by supermarkets to run Price Matching promotions whereby customers can check whether their shop would have been cheaper at a competitor's outlet and, if so, claim a refund or other incentive against the differential.

www.retail100objects.com

Mass Production 1887

Visual Merchandising

RETAILERS RELY ON VISUAL MERCHANDISING TO GENERATE SHOPPER TRAFFIC AND CREATE INTERESTING AND ENJOYABLE STORE ENVIRONMENTS TO PROMOTE PURCHASE BEHAVIOUR. PRESENTING MERCHANDISE IN A COMPELLING MANNER THROUGH A WIDE RANGE OF VISUAL MERCHANDISING TECHNIQUES ALLOWS RETAILERS TO ACHIEVE A WIDE RANGE OF BENEFITS SUCH AS ESTABLISHING PERCEPTIONS RELATING TO PRICE AND MERCHANDISE QUALITY, GENERATING TRIAL USAGE AND ENCOURAGING SHOPPERS TO EXTEND THEIR TIME IN THE STORE.

Visual merchandising has existed since early shopkeepers moved beyond displaying products in a strictly utilitarian fashion on shelves and tables to add a bit of flair to the presentation to heighten the appeal of merchandise. The exact moment in time when this concept emerged is impossible to pinpoint, but generally speaking visual merchandising as it is practised today gained traction at the dawn of the department store era in the early to mid-1800s.

That is when department store operators recognised that one of their key operational challenges was getting shoppers to come in off the busy streets in downtown areas where their stores were typically located. The solution for many was to creating interesting window displays that showcased products in such a way as to inspire and delight passersby to encourage them to come inside the store.

The concept of attractively presenting merchandise extended to inside the store as well. Soon, retailers were relying on visual merchandising to promote sales of new fashions, establish seasonal selling periods, showcase values on key items and help identify key departments.

WHILE THE VISUAL MERCHANDISERS' TOOL KIT HAS EXPANDED CONSIDERABLY IN RECENT DECADES, THE FUNDAMENTAL MOTIVATION OF INCREASING SALES THROUGH THE ARTFUL PRESENTATION OF PRODUCTS REMAINS THE SAME.

As understanding of the powerful effects of visual merchandising grew, retailers began using increasingly elaborate fixtures constructed of wood, glass and metals with various finishes to showcase products. In addition, temporary displays made of corrugated material with elaborate graphics grew increasingly common and the lighting of displays contributed mightily to the effectiveness of visual merchandising.

Today, visual merchandising is an integral component of store design and has grown to encompass other sensory elements such as sound, smell, taste and touch, as well as interactivity. Some retailers also took the concept of visual merchandising to extreme limits with over-the-top store displays that gave rise to the term, "retailtainment."

Contribution to Retail History

The development of visual merchandising practices and their application changed the look of the sales floor and brought a sense of theatre to retail. Through visual merchandising, retailers made shopping fun and brought a sense of discovery to their stores. Retailers found visual merchandising tactics to be equally effective at driving sales of price sensitive of commodity categories and transforming the most discretionary of products into must have items.

Coupon

COUPONS EMERGED AS AN INNOVATIVE MARKETING TACTIC IN THE LATE 1800s AND QUICKLY DEMONSTRATED AN ABILITY TO GENERATE SALES.

THANKS TO THEIR EFFECTIVENESS, COUPONS BECAME AN INDISPENSABLE COMPONENT OF MARKETING STRATEGIES FOR CONSUMER PACKAGED GOODS COMPANIES, AS WELL AS, RETAILERS.

Contribution to Retail History

From their beginning in the late 1800s, coupons proved to be a highly effective tactic to help generate sales. Their usage has become highly refined over the years, but no brand manager would consider launching a new item or promoting an existing product without the humble coupon playing a print or digital role in the promotional mix.

The origins of the first modern coupon can be traced to the Coca-Cola Company. In 1888, the company created a coupon that could be redeemed for a free glass of the new beverage as a means to generate trial and repeat purchase behaviour. In the two decades that followed, the company had redeemed roughly 8.5 million coupons and their usage was credited with launching one of the world's most iconic brands.

Other consumer packaged goods companies took notice of the effectiveness of coupons and before long their usage was widespread. Brand marketers became increasingly sophisticated in their usage of coupons as well, adjusting face values and expirations dates as warranted by economic conditions and shopper sensitivities and deploying coupons as part of an offensive and defensive strategies.

More recently, the traditional physical coupon distributed through magazines, newspapers, direct mail and in store methods, has taken a new form thanks to the advent of digital technology. Brand marketers are now as likely to distribute coupons through email, social media, mobile devices or have incentives directly linked to retailer's loyalty programme to minimise the burden on shoppers to take advantage of the offer. Despite the technological advances, the traditional print coupon remains highly relevant.

Sears Catalogue

IN 1886, RICHARD SEARS, A RAILROAD AGENT IN MINNESOTA, PURCHASED A SHIPMENT OF SURPLUS WATCHES FROM A CHICAGO JEWELLER AND SOLD THEM FOR A PROFIT TO OTHER STATION AGENTS.

STRUCK BY THIS SUCCESS, HE ORDERED MORE GOODS FROM THE JEWELLER FOR RESALE AND BEGAN ADVERTISING HIS JEWELLERY AND WATCHES USING A PRINTED MAILER. THUS BEGAN HIS BUSINESS TO SELL WATCHES THROUGH MAIL ORDER CATALOGUES.

Sears moved to Chicago, Illinois where he met Alvah C. Roebuck who joined him in the business. In 1893 the name of the company was Sears, Roebuck & Co. Julius Rosenwald, a Chicago clothing manufacturer, became a partner in 1895.

The expansion of the US railway system and free postage (in 1896 delivery to US rural areas was free) made the distribution of the Sears Catalogues economical. Sears himself wrote the catalogue; by 1894, it had 322 pages and contained other news items. By 1896, there were Spring and Autumn versions; it became bigger and the company began charging recipients a 25-cent fee. In 1897, colour sections were introduced.

Richard Sears was a good marketer and had an instinct for compelling slogans. For instance: "Book of Bargains: A Money Saver for Everyone" and the "Cheapest Supply House on Earth". The Sears Catalogue also claimed that: "Our trade reaches around the world". Sears also used testimonials from customers, to reassure and confirm that his prices were the lowest and best value.

The list of goods on offer through the catalogue expanded to include sewing machines, sporting goods, musical instruments, saddles, firearms, buggies, bikes, baby carriages, and men's and children's clothing. The 'club order program' encouraged customers to combine their orders with friends or neighbours to share in discounts. By 1898, there were more speciality catalogues – the merchandise reflecting the changes of the time, photo machines, talking machines, and mixed paints.

Ever the entrepreneur, in 1903 Sears was offering "your money back if you are not satisfied" and, to encourage 'customer profit sharing', he gave customers a one-dollar certificate for every dollar spent.

In 1906, Sears opened its catalogue plant and the Sears Merchandise Building Tower, but it was not until 1925 that it began opening physical stores – the first in the Merchandise Building itself. Printed and distributed for 97 years, (the last catalogue was produced in 1993) the Sears Catalogue became widely known as the 'Consumers' Bible'.

Contribution to Retail History

The grand master of mail order, the Sears Catalogue, invented a new category of retailing which was copied and emulated across the world. Responsible for a huge part of the evolution of distance selling, the catalogue can be seen as an early precursor to today's e-commerce retailing.

Bottle

BOTTLES WERE ONCE VALUABLE OBJECTS NOT LIGHTLY DISCARDED. JUST 150 YEARS AGO CARBONATED DRINKS WOULD HAVE BEEN SOLD ON-SITE, IN BARS, SALOONS, TAVERNS AND RESTAURANTS. IF YOU BROUGHT A BOTTLE OF DRINK IT WOULD HAVE BEEN HAND-FILLED AND HAND-CAPPED.

AT THE END OF THE 19TH CENTURY, MASS PRODUCTION ALLOWED FOR GREATER QUANTITIES TO BE SOLD BUT THESE BOTTLES WERE STILL EXPENSIVE SO WERE RETURNABLE IN EXCHANGE FOR A DEPOSIT. THEY HAD A LOGO IMPRINTED INTO THEM SO THAT COMPANIES COULD ENSURE THEY GOT THEIR BOTTLES BACK.

Here we follow the history of just one famous branded bottle – Coca-Cola – one of the most iconic marketing symbols in retail advertising today. Since 1889, the distinct shape and branding of these bottles has made them collector's items.

In 1894, Joseph A. Biedenharn, a shop owner in Mississippi, began bottling Coca-Cola in a glass bottle called a Hutchinson. The drink had sold well in his store. Biedenharn had also sent a case to Asa Griggs Candler, who owned the Coca-Cola Company, but Candler was not interested in bottling – he preferred to focus on fountain sales.

By 1916, Coca-Cola was using a straight-sided bottle but, concerned it wasn't distinctive enough, the company adopted the famous contour shaped bottle (designed by the Root Glass Company of Terre Haute). In 1923, Coca-Cola six packs were introduced, and by 1928, the amount sold in bottles exceeded the amount sold through soda fountains. The Coke bottle was becoming an icon, and in 1950 it appeared on the front cover of TIME Magazine, the first commercial product to do so.

In 2000, in keeping with the ongoing drive for sustainability, Coca-Cola introduced its ultra-glass contour bottle designed for improved impact and resistance, reduced weight and cost. This was both stronger and lighter, saving around 52,000 metric tonnes of glass in one year alone. In 2005 new aluminium contour bottles were introduced.

Contribution to Retail History

Much early commerce was facilitated by the bottle. As an airtight, leakproof container, it enabled distribution of liquid products on an international scale. The returnable deposit scheme was (perhaps inadvertently) an early loyalty and repeat-purchase incentive as customers invariably returned the empty bottles to the store from which they had purchased them and picked up extra items.

Campbell's Soup

CAMPBELL'S SOUP – AND PARTICULARLY ITS BRANDING – HAD A STRONG IMPACT ON AMERICAN POPULAR CULTURE. FAMOUS FOR ITS BRIGHT RED AND WHITE LABEL AND THE 'CHILDREN' (CREATED BY ILLUSTRATOR GRACE WIEDERSEIM DRAYTON), THE BRANDING BECAME EVEN MORE ICONIC WHEN IN 1962, ANDY WARHOL CREATED HIS '32 CAMPBELL SOUP CANS', HERALDING THE ARRIVAL OF POP ART.

DRAYTON DREW FOR CAMPBELL'S ADVERTISING FOR NEARLY TWENTY YEARS. IN THE EARLY DAYS, HER ILLUSTRATIONS USED ON THE LABELS DEPICTED BOYS AND GIRLS, BUT OVER TIME THEY BEGAN TO REPRESENT ADULT PROFESSIONS INCLUDING POLICEMEN, SAILORS, AND SOLDIERS.

Campbell's was a company ahead of its time in terms of production and marketing. John Dorrance, the nephew of Arthur Dorrance, who had taken over the company from Joseph Campbell in 1894, used the knowledge his chemistry degree and PhD gave him to reduce the water content of the company's soups. The condensing saved costs in shipping, packaging, and storage and, in passing some of these savings on to the customers in the form of competitive pricing (a 10oz. can of condensed soup cost a 10 cents whereas a 32oz. can of traditional soup was 30 cents), made Campbell's a household name. By 1922, soup was part and parcel of the American company and Campbell's put "Soup" into its name.

In 1899, when the concept of mass advertising had yet to catch on, Campbell's placed the first advertising on New York City streetcars. Sales of the soup increased by 100% in the City. The first ads included a jingle promoting soup and a large illustration of a red-and-white can of Campbell's soup.

Contribution to Retail History

Campbell's Tomato Soup represents the epitome of branded packaging – a masterful demonstration of how a brand can engage with customers by promoting some of the values it represents visually, (in this case 'home and family'). The packaging also illustrates how branding has to subtly evolve over time, retaining defining characteristics while staying in step with changing consumer tastes and trends.

5

1901 to now

MODERN
SHOPPING

Supermarket

FOOD SHOPPING AND THE RETAIL
INDUSTRY CHANGED FOREVER
WITH THE ADVENT OF THE MODERN
SUPERMARKET IN THE EARLY 1900s.

CONSUMERS RECEPTIVE TO THE CONCEPT
OF SELF-SELECTING FOOD, CONSUMABLES
AND OTHER PRODUCTS ESSENTIAL FOR
DAILY LIVING IN ONE LOCATION ADJUSTED
THEIR PURCHASE PATTERNS AND FUELLED
GROWTH OF THE SUPERMARKET INDUSTRY.

Contribution to Retail History

The supermarket reinvented the food shopping experience by combining under one roof, a wide range of food and non-food products essential to daily living. The approach proved so popular with shoppers that supermarkets would become the dominant retail channel, accounting for the greatest proportion of sales in advanced economies.

Supermarkets represented a new approach to food shopping and shopping in general. As the name implied, the supermarket created a new set of expectations and elevated the store experience for shoppers who were accustomed to the more limited and food-oriented product assortment of traditional grocery stores. The larger format supermarkets were able to elevate the food shopping experience through increased offerings and more appealing merchandise presentations designed to stimulate demand. Supermarkets also satisfied a broader range of shoppers' needs, because they were larger and could allocate the increased selling space to product categories such as household essentials, non-food products, health and beauty aids and ancillary departments such as pharmacies, bakery, floral, banking, dry cleaners and movie rentals.

The combination of product categories, services and store experience proved popular with shoppers who were leading increasingly busy lifestyles and valued the convenience of a retail format that allowed them to satisfy a broader range of needs at a single store.

Supermarkets became the largest single retail channel in advanced economies and their large market share made them a target of competitors. The traditional supermarket industry has come under tremendous pressure, particularly in the United States, where large format stores, known as supercentres, gained favour with shoppers. Additional pressures were exerted as alternative retail channels such as drug stores, dollar stores and hard discount stores with limited assortments and sharp pricing, expanded offerings of food and consumables as a means to generate traffic.

Despite significant challenges in recent decades, the supermarket remains a dominant format characterised by food as its core product offering. The concept of the supermarket continues to evolve to keep pace with shifting family structures and lifestyles that affect consumption patterns. An increased emphasis on the availability of prepared or easy-to-prepare foods at some supermarkets has led to an increasingly blurred distinction between the traditional supermarket and some segments of the food service industry.

"GOING UP!" WE'RE ALL ACCUSTOMED TO DEPARTMENT STORES HAVING FLOOR UPON FLOOR OF PRODUCTS. SPORTSWEAR AND ELECTRICALS IN THE BASEMENT. UP A FLIGHT AND THERE ARE THE COSMETICS ON THE GROUND FLOOR. TRAVEL UP AGAIN AND YOU SEE THE FASHION GOODS AND PERFUMES, MENSWEAR, WOMEN'S WEAR. THE ESCALATOR GAVE BIRTH TO VERTICAL SHOPPING.

IT BEGAN AS A NOVELTY RIDE AT THE OLD IRON PIER AT CONEY ISLAND, NEW YORK, WHEN IN 1896 JESSE RENO PUT PASSENGERS ON A MOVING STAIRWAY THAT TOOK THEM UP ON A CONVEYOR BELT AT A 25-DEGREE ANGLE. HE HAD PATENTED HIS MOVING STAIRS OR INCLINED ELEVATOR IN 1892. A PREVIOUS PATENT HAD BEEN GRANTED IN 1859 (TO NATHAN AMES OF MASSACHUSETTS) FOR A STEAM DRIVEN UNIT CALLED 'REVOLVING STAIRS', BUT THIS WAS NEVER BUILT.

In 1897, along came another inventor, Charles Seeberger, with a revamp. His word for his moving stairs – 'escalator' – came from the Latin 'scala', meaning steps. In 1899, Seeberger started working with the Otis Elevator Company to get his first commercial escalators into production at the Otis factory in Yonkers, New York. In 1900, the wooden escalator they had created won first prize at the Exposition Universelle in Paris.

Meanwhile, Jesse Reno was still working on his own designs and in 1902 founded the Reno Electric Stairways and Conveyors Company. Both Reno and Seeberger sold their patents to the Otis Elevator Company. The company's engineers, led by David Lindquist, upgraded the Reno and Seeberger designs by creating the 'cleated' level steps of the modern escalator that we still see in our stores and shopping malls today.

Modern escalators have single-piece aluminium or stainless steel steps that move on a system of tracks in a continuous loop, with moving handrails that keep pace with the movement of the stairs. Designs vary according to how many people they are expected to transport. A single-width escalator travelling at 1.5 feet or 0.46 metres per second can move an estimated 170 people every five minutes.

Contribution to Retail History

Being able to move a large volume of people around a store and up and down shopping mall level, with ease and in comfort, helps encourage sales. But it's not just about mobility. Escalators are invariably located in the centre of the store or mall and provide customers with a bird's-eye view of merchandise, optimising the retailers' opportunity to promote goods and offers. Today, stores are installing escalators designed to take a shopping trolley so that customers can keep their purchase with them as they journey through the store.

Air Conditioning

THE DESIRE TO BE ABLE TO CHILL THE TEMPERATURE OF THE IMMEDIATE SURROUNDINGS CAN BE TRACED BACK FOR CENTURIES; ANCIENT EGYPTIANS, ANCIENT ROMANS AND THE HAN DYNASTY IN 2ND CENTURY CHINA ALL TRIED VARIOUS WAYS TO COOL THE AIR AROUND THEM.

THE FATHER OF MODERN AIR CONDITIONING, HOWEVER, WAS AN AMERICAN CORNELL UNIVERSITY GRADUATE, WILLIS HAVILAND CARRIER. THE FIRST AIR CONDITIONING UNIT, DESIGNED AND BUILT BY HIM IN BUFFALO, BEGAN OPERATION IN JULY 1902. IN 1906, HE LODGED HIS FIRST PATENT FOR 'THE APPARATUS FOR TREATING AIR'.

Five years later, in 1911, Carrier told the American Society of Mechanical Engineers about his new formula for calculating air conditions. He said he had worked it out while waiting for a train on a foggy night, and that by the time the train arrived at the station, he had understood the dynamics between temperature, humidity and dew point. That formula is still in use today.

Controlling humidity levels before and after production, led to improvements in many products including, film, tobacco, processed meats, medical capsules and certain textiles. In 1921, Carrier patented his centrifugal refrigeration machine. It was the first practical method for cooling large spaces and it was a safer and more efficient method for chilling air.

Three years later, several Carrier centrifugal chillers were installed in the JL Hudson Department Store in Detroit, Michigan. Shoppers loved to shop in the new 'air conditioned' stores and not surprisingly, the movie theatres were the next to install them. In 1928 the Carrier systems began being installed in domestic homes, now under the name residential "Weathermaker".

Contribution to Retail History

Today, the retail experience remains reliant on air conditioning to create a 'chilled' environment, persuading shoppers to stay in stores longer and keeping merchandise fresh along the supply chain. The shoppers in the 'meccas' of the malls of places like Las Vegas, Dubai and Singapore owe a debt of gratitude to Carrier's genius.

Clothes Hanger

WHATEVER TYPE OF CLOTHES HANGER WE USE TODAY — METAL, WOOD OR PLASTIC — IT DRAPES OUR SHIRTS, BLOUSES, JACKETS, TROUSERS, SKIRTS, AS IF THE CLOTHES WERE SITTING ON OUR OWN 'HUMAN' SHOULDERS.

ROW AFTER ROW OF CLOTHES SIT ON THESE HUMBLE HANGERS, READY FOR US TO PURCHASE THROUGHOUT STORES ALL OVER THE WORLD.

Contribution to Retail History

Use of hangers enabled retailers to easily move and display rails of clothing at any given location on the shop floor. Garments were displayed with more efficient use of store space and to far better effect — uncreased, and more accessible to browsing customers, making it easy for them to see what was in style and in stock and encouraging closer scrutiny and handling. The clothes hanger also enabled more efficient distribution of merchandise between the manufacturer and the store.

In 1903, Albert J. Parkhouse, heard his co-worker at the Timberlake Wire and Novelty Company in Jackson, Michigan, complain that there were not enough hooks to put his coat on and set about solving the problem. Parkhouse bent a piece of wire into two ovals, with ends twisted together to form a hook. The first recorded retail use of the early hangers was in 1906 in Grand Rapids, Michigan, when Meyer May, a men's clothier, was the first to use them to put his merchandise on.

Parkhouse did patent his invention, but he was not actually the first. That credit goes to O. A. North of Connecticut, who in 1869, took out a clothes hook patent. (It should also be acknowledged that some histories credit the US President, Thomas Jefferson, with inventing the first wooden hanger.)

In fact, in the USA, there have been many patents for various types of clothes hangers; over 200 have been counted to date.

The Parkhouse wire clothes hook was further improved in 1932 when Schuyler C. Hulett received a patent for putting cardboard tubes onto the upper and lower portions of the hook, so that when freshly washed clothes were put over them they did not crease. In 1935, the next evolution was seen in the form of a hanger with a tube on the lower bar, the invention of Elmer D. Rogers.

Over the years, hangers have become carriers for the name of the brands as well as the clothes themselves, but the basic principles of their design have remained pretty much the same. They remain an excellent example of form following function.

HOLLOWED WOOD, WOVEN GRASSES, SHELLS, LEAVES AND EVEN ANIMAL ORGANS WERE USED AS THE EARLIEST FORM OF PACKAGING. THEN CAME METALS, POTTERY AND PAPER. PLASTIC, FIRST DEVELOPED IN THE 19TH CENTURY, HAS PROVED TO BE ONE OF THE MOST ADAPTABLE AND DURABLE FORMS OF PACKAGING.

Plastic Packaging

The substance Styrene was first distilled from a balsam tree in 1831 but the products made from it were brittle and broke easily. In 1862, the first man-made plastic was unveiled by Alexander Parkes at the Great International Exhibition in London. The material was derived from cellulose and called Parkesine. When heated, it could be moulded to shape, which it then retained when cold.

In 1870 (during the American Civil War), a New York engineer, John Wesley Hyatt and his brother, Isaiah Smith Hyatt, created and patented 'celluloid'. It could be carved and shaped rather than moulded. Some thirty years later, a Swiss textile engineer, Dr Jacque Edwin Brandenberger, created cellophane. It was flexible, and water resistant. Cellophane Tape followed and then Saran™, it's 'clinging' qualities saw it first used to protect military equipment and later for food packaging. In the 1930s, German manufacturers refined the early Styrene processes and foam packaging materials were available worldwide from the 1950s.

Plastic bottle production remained relatively expensive, until the 1960s when manufacturing techniques changed and high-density polyethylene was introduced. The plastic bottles created from it were cheaper to produce and lighter than glass bottles.

ENGLISH

⚠ **WARNING!**
SUFFOCATION HAZARD
- Keep plastic bags away from babies and children.

Contribution to Retail History

With the capacity to be moulded into any form, plastic provides all the flexibility required to create packaging for goods of all shapes and sizes. Lightweight, it provided manufacturers with a cost-effective packaging method for distribution. Being airtight, watertight and able to withstand freezing temperatures, the introduction of plastic packaging greatly extended the shelf life – and therefore geographic footprint – of perishable goods. The advent of the microwave extended the power of plastic packaging even further, opening up an entirely new concept in home cooking, the microwaveable 'ready meal'.

Float and Armoured Glass

WE CALL IT 'WINDOW SHOPPING'. WE WALK ALONG THE HIGH STREET, STARE AT THE CLOTHES OR OTHER PRODUCTS IN THE WINDOWS, BUT PROBABLY TAKE FOR GRANTED THE GLAZING THROUGH WHICH WE'RE GAZING. HOWEVER, THE ALLURE OF THE ARTFULLY ARRANGED WINDOW DISPLAYS THAT DRAW US IN TO SPEND MONEY ONLY WORKS BECAUSE OF THE DEVELOPMENTS IN GLASS-MAKING TECHNIQUES THAT MADE SUCH 'WALLS' OF GLASS POSSIBLE.

In the late 17th century, the French began using grinding and polishing techniques to produce the first plate glass, but at that time it was something only the rich could aspire to own. The French Revolution and the English Industrial Revolution coincided with a revolution in glass manufacturing, using compressed air to produce better, flatter, glass panes.

By the 1860s, store and office buildings were using plate glass. In the 20th century, machines could produce sheet after sheet of flat glass for windows. That glass became stronger and tints were applied. In 1903, bullet proof glass was 'accidentally' discovered when a French chemist, Edouard Benedictus, dropped a glass beaker on the floor. It didn't break completely apart as it was coated with plastic cellulose nitrate.

When Henry Gordon Selfridge came to build his Oxford Street store in the early 1900s, he invested £400,000 (a small fortune) acquiring a series of Georgian buildings and turning them into a steel framed, five-storey department store. The store opened in 1909, complete with cast iron window frames and glass windows measuring over 19 feet by 12 feet. A revelation, now passers-by were confronted with merchandise displays that drew them in. 'Lifestyle' tableaux, seasonal goods, working televisions – the windows provided a 3D advertising hoarding.

In the 1950s Sir Alistair Pilkington and Kenneth Bickerstaff, developed the 'float' glass manufacturing technique (produced by heating a furnace to 1500°C and then allowing the molten liquid inside the furnace to flow through molten tin). The molten glass floats because the density of materials is different and it is this technique that gives the flatness to the surface of the glass. This float glass became commercially successful during the 1960s and is still manufactured and in use across the world today.

www.retail100objects.com

Contribution to Retail History

The shop window displays made possible by these glazing techniques became key to the retailers' ability to persuade passing trade to step through the door. In the age of online shopping, the role of window merchandising is even more vital. Since many customers go out as much to browse as to buy, the power of attraction rests heavily on the view through the window. Today, glass has become a key component of retail architecture for some brands – witness Apple stores' use of it as a central tenet of their retail design philosophy.

Selfridge's Lavatory

IN THE MID-19TH CENTURY, THE CONCEPT OF ONE-STOP SHOPPING IN THE FORM OF THE DEPARTMENT STORE, GALLERIA AND ARCADE ARRIVED. THESE PLACES WERE DESTINATIONS IN THEIR OWN RIGHT, OFFERING A SHOPPING ENVIRONMENT THAT RESPECTABLE PEOPLE WERE KEEN TO EXPERIENCE.

THE NEW WELL-OFF URBAN POPULATION WAS ATTRACTED IN THEIR THOUSANDS, NOT JUST TO SHOP, BUT ALSO TO SOCIALISE, OFTEN SPENDING THE ENTIRE DAY OUT IN THE PROCESS. BUT, IF RESPECTABLE PERSONS WERE TO BE ENCOURAGED TO DWELL, SHOP, AND MINGLE, WHERE WERE THEY TO ANSWER THE INEVITABLE CALL OF NATURE?

At this time, no real provision was made for women; they trained themselves not to need to use facilities when away from the domestic environment and if they really had to do so, they excused themselves from company and managed as best they could, with non-existent, or at best, primitive amenities. All this was changed with the arrival in London at the turn of the century of Gordon Harry Selfridge.

Harry was determined to build the best store in the world; he already had 30 odd years' experience in Chicago running Marshall Fields, at that time probably the number one Department Store in the US.

Harry Selfridge positively encouraged customers to spend as long as they wanted in the store, with free entrance, impressive window displays, touchable merchandise, longer opening hours and the widest range of merchandise and store services yet available. But as well as being a great merchant, Selfridge understood that in-store services would also be key to happy customers. So, he invested behind the scenes, not least by providing what were really the first public in-store lavatories for men and women. A long established competitor of Selfridges, Whiteleys in Bayswater, did provide some toilet facilities, but these were private, for customers only and were very rudimentary affairs. Not so at Selfridges, where, by the standards of the day, the facilities were lavish, with enclosed cubicles, wash basins with hot water, easy chairs, mirrors and attendants to help. And importantly, given the stores dictum of 'spend all day here, and you don't have to buy anything', the lavatories were public.

Contribution to Retail History

The public lavatories were an innovation that was hugely welcomed by the public. Important as they were in their own right, the lavatories were also a demonstration of an emerging 'customer services' retail ethos — something that has continued to define and differentiate retail brands ever since.

www.retail100objects.com

Allen Key

THE ALLEN KEY (OR WRENCH) IS A BRAND NAME WE HAVE ALL BECOME FAMILIAR WITH. WE USE THESE HEX KEYS TO SCREW AND SECURE VARIOUS DEVICES BUT MOST COMMONLY WE REACH FOR THEM WHEN WE TAKE HOME, UNPACK AND NEED TO SELF-ASSEMBLE OUR DIY FURNITURE.

AROUND 1911, THE STANDARD PRESSED STEEL COMPANY (AN AMERICAN MANUFACTURER WHICH MADE SHAFT HANGERS AND COLLARS USING SET SCREWS) IS SAID TO HAVE FIRST USED THE 'UNBREAKABLE' SCREW.

At that time known as the 'Unbrako', it became a world leader in its mass production. The founder of SPS was Howard T. Hallowell, Senior. He wrote: "For a while we experimented with a screw containing a square hole like the English screw, but soon found these would not be acceptable in this country, the US. Then we decided to incorporate a hexagon socket into the screw." He called his method 'the internal-wrenching hexagon drive.'

These headless set screws were well received by safety campaigners, who were keen to see them used on the pulleys and shafts in factories at that time. Headless screws were less likely to catch the clothing of workers and risk pulling them onto the running shafts.

At around the same time (1909 – 1910), William G. Allen had patented a method of 'cold-forming' screw heads around a hexagonal die. We don't know if Hallowell used this same method or some other for his screws. Advertisements for the 'Allen safety set screw' were published by the Allen Manufacturing Company of Connecticut from 1910. The company trade marked the name 'Allen wrench or key' for its range of hex wrenches in 1943. The trade mark is now owned by the Apex Tool Group.

In the Second World War the push for more production of every kind saw hex or Allen keys come into even wider use. Popular science magazine wrote in 1946: "Cap screws and set screws with heads recessed to take hexagonal-bar wrenches are coming into increasing use." The popularity of the Allen key continued to grow and it is now sold in different sizes in countries all over the world.

Contribution to Retail History

The humble Allen key facilitated a boom in the sale of flat packed goods for home assembly and resulted in the emergence of a new kind of DIY store, of which IKEA is the best recognised across the world. From its first stores in Scandinavia in the 1960s, IKEA spread its revolutionary retail model across Europe and the US during the 1970s and 1980s and then into China, which is now its second largest market. Today, throughout its 400 plus stores across 31 countries, customers are navigated through 'room sets' that sell a lifestyle they – with the help of an Allen Key – can re-create, relatively cheaply and easily, in their own home.

Neon Lighting

NEON COMES FROM THE GREEK 'NEOS' MEANING 'THE NEW GAS'. WILLIAM RAMSEY AND M. W. TRAVERS IN LONDON DISCOVERED NEON GAS, IN 1898. IT IS MADE BY LIQUEFYING AIR AND IT IS SEPARATED FROM OTHER GASES BY FRACTIONAL DISTILLATION.

THE FRENCH ENGINEER AND CHEMIST, GEORGES CLAUDE, WAS THE FIRST PERSON TO APPLY AN ELECTRICAL DISCHARGE TO A SEALED TUBE OF NEON GAS TO CREATE A LIGHT, AND HIS FIRST NEON LAMP WAS UNVEILED IN 1910, IN PARIS. HE PATENTED HIS NEON LIGHTING TUBE IN THE UNITED STATES, IN 1915.

The application of Claude's new technology quickly followed. His company, Claude Neon, sold two neon gas signs to a Packard car dealership in Los Angeles in 1923. The signs said 'Packard' and each sign cost $1,250. The idea quickly took off and others began using neon lighting (nicknamed 'liquid fire') for their outdoor advertising too. By 1924, Claude Neon franchises had appeared in 14 major cities across the US, and in 1927, the company could claim that it had created 611 out of the 750 neon signs on display in New York City.

After the Second World War, plexiglas shadow boxes with fluorescent lighting displaying letters and graphics, took over from neon. In the US, many neon signs were switched off during the wartime blackout period and were never switched back on again.

However, from the late 1970s, a neon revival began and today retailers and advertisers continue to harness its appeal as a material for signage. From Times Square in New York, to Piccadilly Circus in London, to the Akihabara district of Tokyo, brands and retail outlets use neon to arrest the attention of passers-by. Architects and merchandisers incorporate neon to add illustrative flourishes to the interior and exterior of buildings – from simple 'open/closed' signs to artistic creations that create unique abstract sculptures by 'drawing' with light.

Contribution to Retail History

Neon signs broke new ground in retail advertising and transformed the urban landscape at night. Eye-catching and adaptable, the tubes are bent by hand. Neon signage continues to lend itself to use for logos and information signage and ambitious art installations.

Shopping Bag

ONE OBSERVANT MINNESOTA GROCERY STORE OWNER, WALTER H. DEUBNER, WANTED TO INCREASE TRADE AT HIS STORE. HE NOTICED THAT WHAT PEOPLE PURCHASED WAS LIMITED BY WHAT THEY COULD CARRY.

FOUR YEARS LATER, HE HAD DEVELOPED A PREFABRICATED INEXPENSIVE PACKAGE – A PAPER BAG WITH A CORD RUNNING THROUGH IT. THIS 'DEUBNER SHOPPING BAG' WAS EASY TO USE AND STRONG ENOUGH TO CARRY UP TO SEVENTY-FIVE POUNDS OF GROCERIES. THE BAGS COST FIVE CENTS EACH. DEUBNER PATENTED HIS BAG IN 1912 AND WITHIN THREE YEARS, HE WAS SELLING OVER A MILLION SHOPPING BAGS A YEAR.

The inventor of the modern lightweight plastic shopping bag was the Swedish engineer, Sten Gustaf Thulin. He created a bag, made in one piece from a flat tube of plastic for the packaging company Celloplast, who patented it worldwide in 1965. It was strong and could carry a lot. The company was a pioneer in plastics processing and expanded across Europe and the US to manufacture shopping bags. The US petrochemicals group, Mobil, overturned Celloplast's US patent in 1977.

The Dixie Bag Company, of Georgia, the Houston Poly Bag and Capitol Poly all developed the manufacturing techniques further and grocery chains began to use plastic (or polyethylene) bags instead of paper ones. By the mid 1980s, plastic bags were being used to carry shopping by consumers the world over.

Often referred to as the 'single use bag', what was once a benefit has since become a hindrance. Environmental concerns impact upon the plastic bag industry, with between 500 billion and 1 trillion plastic bags being used each year globally. A contributor to roadside litter, they can take centuries to decompose.

Contribution to Retail History

Polythene shopping bags increased the average transaction value by enabling customers to purchase and transport more products. The bags also provided a relatively cheap but highly visible way for retailers to promote their brand. In recent years, retailers have encouraged customers to move towards a 'bag for life' system to improve the rate of re-use.

FROM THE MID-20TH CENTURY, HOME DELIVERY OF RETAIL GOODS BECAME COMMON ACROSS THE DEVELOPED WORLD. PERISHABLE PRODUCTS SUCH AS MILK, EGGS, FRUIT AND VEGETABLES WERE DELIVERED WEEKLY OR EVEN DAILY TO CUSTOMERS BY LOCAL FARMS AND SUPPLIERS.

Delivery Van

Contribution to Retail History

From mobile shops, to basic supply chain fulfilment and on to their vital role in today's e-commerce delivery, the humble van or truck has been the very bedrock of retail. The modern supply chain is founded on trucks and vans, with only international supply relying on other forms of transport such as plane and ship.

AS WELL AS DELIVERING TO ORDER (SUCH AS THE DAILY MILK ROUND), GROCERS, BAKERS, FISHMONGERS AND OTHERS WOULD DRIVE THEIR VANS FROM PLACE TO PLACE (TO A REGULAR SCHEDULE), PARK UP AND SELL BEFORE MOVING ON TO THE NEXT DESTINATION.

It was the Ford Model T that first brought the delivery van within the reach of high street businesses (the American Messenger Company in Seattle, Washington, founded by James Casey, started using its first Model T delivery car in 1913), followed by the purpose built light vans, after 1945. The first generation of compact vans appeared in the US in the 1960s, borrowing their design from the Volkswagen Bus. They were called 'step vans' because a deliveryman could step-up into one via low van steps built under the doors. It became a standard truck type widely used by delivery services, courier companies and parcel post.

The growth in private car ownership, coupled with the advent of the supermarket and out-of-town retail shopping centres, saw a decline in use of the van for home delivery services during the last quarter of the 20th century. However, the past decade has seen a resurgence in use as the massive growth of online shopping has reinstated the delivery van in its pivotal position at the end of the retail distribution chain.

Calculator

IN 1642, A FRENCHMAN, BLAISE PASCAL, INVENTED THE 'PASCALINE' – A MECHANICAL CALCULATOR THAT COULD ADD, SUBTRACT, MULTIPLY AND DIVIDE.

HOWEVER, IT WAS NOT UNTIL NEARLY 200 YEARS LATER THAT THE PRINCIPLES OF THE MECHANICAL CALCULATOR WERE ADAPTED AND ADOPTED FOR COMMERCIAL USE.

The Arithmometer, invented in 1820 and produced in 1851, became the first real success story. By 1890, around 2,500 devices had been sold. The manufacturing boom of the Industrial Revolution allowed better models to be produced en masse. Between 1820 and 1914 the calculator went from being something that only the rich could afford, to being heavily used in commercial environments.

In 1902, James L. Dalton (an American), made a new push-button design and called it the 'Dalton Adding Machine'. In 1948, the Curta calculator was developed. It was small and portable enough to hold in your hand. In the 1950s and 1960s, as computer technology developed, so too did calculators, and increasingly they were built into machines.

The first prototype of a hand-held calculator was developed by Texas Instruments in 1967 and was called 'Cal Tech'. By 1970, the Japanese were making the first portable calculators which incorporated rechargeable batteries and used just a few chips of low power consumption. Today, calculators are ubiquitous, found in every device and enabling instant calculation anywhere.

Contribution to Retail History

Calculators expedited accounting processes throughout the supply chain. Retailers were no longer at the mercy of the numeracy of their cashiers as all the additions and subtractions for working out change was done for them. Customers could better calculate and manage the cost of their shopping as they filled their baskets or trolleys and could also work out what deals and offers (for example, '15% off') would save them in monetary terms. The speed and accuracy of the checkout process greatly improved the overall customer experience.

Checkout

THE MODERN CHECKOUT, CONSISTING OF A PAYMENT PROCESSING STATION STAFFED BY A CASHIER, IS A FOUNDATIONAL ELEMENT OF THE SELF-SERVICE RETAIL EXPERIENCE THAT ROSE TO PROMINENCE IN THE EARLY 1900s.

THE RETAIL INDUSTRY IS DEPENDENT ON PROPERLY FUNCTIONING CHECKOUTS WITH BILLIONS OF TRANSACTIONS PROCESSED AT MILLIONS OF MERCHANT LOCATIONS WORLDWIDE EVERY DAY.

The concept of the checkout has existed since buyers and sellers first completed transactions at centralised locations. Early checkouts of the modern retail era were manual, requiring cashiers to key prices and process payments that were made by cash, cheque or early forms of credit. As retailing advanced to the chain store age, the modern checkout emerged to define the customer experience and play an important role in the industry's development.

It was the development of the barcode that significantly revolutionised the checkout by improving speed, accuracy and ease of use for shoppers and retail cashiers. Retailers who embraced the technology gained an important competitive advantage and came to recognise the powerful impact the checkout could have on shoppers' perceptions of the store experience. As such, the checkout became the focus of intense process improvement efforts and innovations. The conveyor belt and bagging turnstiles were introduced to accelerate throughput.

Retailers' efforts to minimise shoppers' waiting times also led to the introduction of express lanes for use by those with a limited number of items or guarantees that additional checkout lanes would be opened if the number of people in line exceeded a certain amount.

More recently, the checkout has continued to evolve thanks to technological advancements and checkout configurations that enable shoppers to self-scan merchandise without the aid of cashiers. Likewise, the growth of e-commerce has introduced a new type of digital check where the principles of speed, accuracy and ease of use remain equally relevant. Newer advancements on the digital front are facilitating a range of mobile checkout possibilities that represent the next stage of evolution for the checkout.

Contribution to Retail History

Centralised checkouts gave retailers the ability to quickly and accurately tally customers' purchases and process payments. The checkout contributed to the rise of self-service retail and reshaped shoppers' expectations of the store experience. As such, it became a key consideration in store design and exerted a powerful influence on decisions relating to operations, marketing and merchandising.

www.retail100objects.com

Conveyor Belt

CONVEYOR BELTS BEGAN IN THE LATTER HALF OF THE 17TH CENTURY, DEVISED AS A WAY OF MOVING GRAIN SACKS OVER SHORT DISTANCES. THEY WORKED BY ALLOWING A BELT MADE OF LEATHER, CANVAS OR RUBBER TO TRAVEL OVER A FLAT WOODEN BED.

BY THE BEGINNING OF THE 20TH CENTURY, THEIR USAGE AND DEVELOPMENT WAS MORE WIDESPREAD.

In 1908, Hymle Goddard of the Logan Company was the first to receive the patent for the roller conveyor but it did not do well. In 1919, powered and free conveyors were used in automotive production and then in coal mines. In the Second World War, synthetic conveyor belts (PVC and rubber) were introduced. During the second half of the 20th century, engineers perfected internally powered conveyor rollers and motorised pulleys that eliminated costly maintenance procedures.

The conveyor belt rapidly became an integral component of virtually every stage of the retail supply chain. Conveyor belts transport raw materials from the point of extraction. Production assembly lines use them to choreograph and conduct the process of making, assembling and checking goods. Within the retail environment, conveyor belts are essential to delivering a streamlined checkout process. Warehouse and distribution centres rely on them to move stock in and out.

Contribution to Retail History

By merging the mechanisation of the conveyor belt with computer control systems, retail distribution centre operations around the globe have become faster and more efficient and have been able to achieve huge savings in labour costs.

Shopping Centre

THE SHOPPING CENTRE IS A CONCEPT AS OLD AS COMMERCE ITSELF AS EARLY MERCHANTS WERE QUICK TO RECOGNISE THE VALUE OF GATHERING AT A CENTRALISED LOCATION TO PEDDLE THEIR WARES.

THEN, AS NOW, THE FOUNDATIONAL SUCCESS OF THE SHOPPING CENTRE LIES IN ITS POWERFUL APPEAL AS A DESTINATION WHERE SHOPPERS CAN SATISFY A WIDE RANGE OF NEEDS AND WANTS FOR PRODUCTS AND SERVICES.

Shopping centres perfectly illustrate the adage that the whole is greater than the sum of its parts. Physically locating numerous retail stores at a single location made the shopping centre a compelling destination. In turn, retailers' prospects for success improved because they benefited from higher levels of shopper traffic than they could have generated independently. In addition, for retailers who occupied shopping centres, a host of business considerations were simplified or eliminated. Unlike operators of standalone stores, shopping centre tenants were freed from issues related to real estate site selection, construction and a host of operational and maintenance considerations.

The forerunner of the modern shopping centre is recognised as the Country Club Plaza, developed by the J.C. Nichols Company near Kansas City, Missouri, in 1922. Three decades later in 1954, the concept of the shopping centre experienced a major turning point with the opening of the first enclosed mall called 'Southdale' near Minneapolis, Minnesota.

Enclosed malls were incredibly popular. The mall became a retail phenomenon and from the 1960s through the 1980s, enclosed malls grew rapidly and transformed the retail landscape.

As mall developers strived to create ever more powerful destinations, mega malls, such as the West Edmonton Mall in Alberta, Canada and the Mall of America in Minneapolis, emerged in the 1980s. These structures broke new ground in the world of shopping centre development by including food, entertainment and amusement options among their extensive retail offerings. The combination elevated the mega mall to the status of tourist destination.

While the word "mall" has become synonymous with shopping centre, retail destinations today take many different forms and go by names such as strip centre, power centre, outlet mall or lifestyle centre. Their approach to site selection, architectural design and tenant mix, varies. Each relies on the fundamental principle that retailers' exponentially increase their prospects for success when assembled together to create a shopping centre.

Contribution to Retail History

The shopping centre represented the earliest form of retail development and established the philosophy that a mutually beneficial effect was created by assembling a group of retailers together to form a destination. This foundational principle shaped shopping centre development over the centuries and continues to do so today. The enduring appeal of the shopping centre lies in its ability to evolve the tenant mix to provide the most relevant offering of products and services to secure the shopping centre's status as a local, regional or global destination.

Tannoy

WHILE TANNOY IS WIDELY USED AS MEANING A GENERIC PUBLIC ADDRESS SYSTEM IT IS IN FACT A TRADE MARK BELONGING TO TANNOY, A SCOTTISH-BASED MANUFACTURER OF LOUDSPEAKERS AND PUBLIC ADDRESS SYSTEMS, FIRST ESTABLISHED IN 1926.

HOWEVER, THE FIRST WORKING PA SYSTEM WAS INVENTED IN THE UNITED STATES BY EDWIN JENSEN AND PETER PRIDHAM. IN 1915, THEIR COMPANY, MAGNAVOX, CREATED THE FIRST EVER DYNAMIC LOUDSPEAKER. PRIOR TO THAT, PA SYSTEMS WERE IN EFFECT, JUST A FUNNEL OR BULLHORN WITHOUT ANY FORM OF ELECTRONIC AMPLIFICATION.

Amplified PA systems underwent rapid development during the Second World War. In the UK, Tannoy became a household name. These days, the word Tannoy is synonymous with sound, appearing in the dictionary as: 'a communications system with loudspeakers, used for making announcements in public buildings.' The phrase 'Over the Tannoy' is universally used to describe a PA announcement.

Contribution to Retail History

As supermarkets and retail outlets expanded and developed enormous footprints, the deployment of PA (or 'Tannoy') systems in stores became standard. Amplified sound enabled management to direct operations. For example, additional staff to occupy checkouts, clean spillages or report to another member of the team could be called so that the supervisor didn't have to travel the entire shop floor. The system also enabled the introduction of piped 'muzak' throughout the retail environment, creating a more convivial shopping ambience. The PA's potential as a communication media for tactical promotions was also quickly seized upon, enabling announcements regarding special offers and sampling opportunities to be broadcast to every customer at once, irrespective of their location within the store.

THE FAMOUS WRIGHT BROTHERS, ORVILLE AND WILBUR, MADE THE FIRST SUCCESSFUL EXPERIMENTAL FLIGHT ON 17 DECEMBER 1903, IN WHICH THEIR AKA AEROPLANE TOOK OFF AND LANDED WITH A MAN ON BOARD. IN THE FIRST OF THREE FLIGHTS THAT DAY, THEIR AEROPLANE FLEW TO AN ALTITUDE OF 10 FEET, TRAVELLED 120 FEET, AND LANDED 12 SECONDS AFTER TAKE-OFF.

Aeroplane

DURING THE FIRST HALF OF THE 20TH CENTURY, INNOVATIONS IN FLIGHT AND PLANE DESIGN BLOSSOMED, ACHIEVING ANOTHER KEY LANDMARK WITH THE DEVELOPMENT OF THE JET ENGINE IN THE LATE 1930s BY TWO ENGINEERS: FRANK WHITTLE OF THE UK AND HANS VON OHAIN OF GERMANY. IN THE SECOND HALF OF THE 20TH CENTURY, IT WAS THE PASSENGERS AND THE TOURIST INDUSTRY THAT BEGAN TO REAP THE REWARDS OF MODERN FLIGHT.

In 1969, the Boeing 747 was unveiled and in the same year the Aerospatiale-BAC Concorde supersonic passenger airliner made its maiden flight. The Boeing 747 was the largest commercial passenger aircraft ever to fly. It still carries millions of passengers each year, but it has now been overtaken in size by the Airbus A380. A double-decker, wide-body, four-engine jet airliner, the Airbus A380 is the world's biggest passenger airliner. Many airports have had to upgrade their facilities to accommodate it because of its size.

Tourism is now an essential activity for many economies and the business travel audience also accounts for a significant percentage of travel, as we become an increasingly global economy. In 2011, there were over 983 million international tourist arrivals worldwide and numbers are set to rise. No previous generations have been able to travel so freely and so widely.

Contribution to Retail History

Air travel opened shoppers' eyes to wider retail horizons; package holidays took them to new places and soon the relative speed and ease of flight prompted people to cross continents just to shop. For the supply and distribution chain, aeroplanes opened up a world of opportunity – literally. The ability to airfreight fresh goods and have them arrive at their destination in hours transformed the supermarket shelves, the concept of seasonality, and the shopping habits of consumers

Kvass Barrel

KVASS HAS BEEN ENJOYED IN RUSSIA AND ACROSS PARTS OF EASTERN EUROPE FOR CENTURIES, BY EVERY SOCIAL GROUP FROM TSARS TO PEASANTS.

EVEN TODAY, IN THE SUMMER YOU WILL SEE PEOPLE LINING UP TO PURCHASE A GLASS OF THIS TANGY BEVERAGE FROM THE STREET VENDOR'S BARREL.

Kvass is a drink made from stale, dark, sourdough rye bread. It's brown and bubbly, with a beer-like taste, but its alcohol content is so low (less than 1%) that it's considered non-alcoholic (although if left to ferment for long enough, the alcohol content will increase). It might be flavoured with herbs, strawberries, raisins, currants, lemons, cherries, apples or mint. Hailed as one of the most thirst-quenching drinks available, Kvass is also considered to offer health benefits too, acting as both an isotonic and probiotic.

Kvass was often made at home; commercial production of it only began in the late 19th century. But, such is the product's short shelf life (just a few days) it was frequently sold on the street, directly out of bright yellow mobile, barrel-shaped tanks. Customers would queue up to buy it by the glass, or in larger volumes, decanting it from the tank into the vessels they had brought from home.

Contribution to Retail History

In the Soviet economy, the sale of goods was a centralised process. Items and produce were brought to central depots for distribution through specific points of sale. In direct contrast, the Kvass barrel, alongside the beer barrel, was a way of distributing a high demand, perishable product quickly and efficiently, on every street corner, creating a myriad of 'pop up' retail distribution points. An important example of street vending in the Soviet Union, the Kvass barrel paved the way for other goods to be sold in this way, with numerous mobile food and drink vending points throughout streets of Russian cities, e.g. chains like Kroshka-Kartoshka or Steff.

Avoska Shopping Bag

IT LOOKS LIKE A BASKETBALL NET, BUT IN FACT, IT'S A BAG, WIDELY USED BY RUSSIAN SHOPPERS (BOTH WOMEN AND MEN) SINCE THE 1930s

THE STRING BAG SCRUNCHES UP INTO SOMETHING THAT FITS INTO YOUR PALM, AND IS EASILY PUT IN A HANDBAG OR BRIEFCASE WHEN YOU LEAVE FOR WORK. WHEN YOU LATER GO TO SHOP, YOU HAVE A ROBUST, CAPACIOUS GROCERY BAG.

The Avoska bag dates back to 1935 and the word avos means 'maybe' or 'perhaps' in Russian. At that time in the USSR, many goods were scarce so the sentiment was apt. People carried the string bags everywhere in the hope of being able to use them to scoop up large quantities of products that, with luck, they might come across being sold. The popular Russian comedian, Akrady Raikin used to joke about his 'maybe' bag... "Here's my maybe-bag. Maybe I'll get something into it."

In the 1970s Soviet consumers spent hundreds of hours of their lives waiting in line to buy goods. They were well versed in 'impulse' buying, in that if they saw a queue forming, it was standard procedure to join it and only then enquire about what was being sold. The uncertainty of what goods would be available, when and where, instilled in people an instinct to stockpile. This is where the Avoska bag was so useful. When goods suddenly appeared in a shop or a market, the expanding string bag enabled the shopper to stock up in bulk at a moment's notice.

Contribution to Retail History

The Avoska bag was a major cultural phenomenon of everyday Soviet life, symbolising the ongoing struggle of sourcing and purchasing everyday consumer goods. In recent years, the principle of the Avoska bag has begun to be applied in the West but it is prompted by a different concern — shoppers have begun to carry 'fold away' shopping bags with them to reduce the use of plastic carrier bags.

Price Gun

THE INVENTION OF THE PRICE GUN MARKED A STEP FORWARD IN RETAIL EFFICIENCY BY ENABLING STORE PERSONNEL TO QUICKLY AND ACCURATELY PRICE MERCHANDISE.

THE IMPROVEMENT IN PRICE TRANSPARENCY INSTILLED CONFIDENCE IN SHOPPERS AND SIMPLIFIED THE CHECKOUT PROCESS FOR CASHIERS.

The price gun was invented in 1935 by Ray Stanton "Stan" Avery who worked as a retail clerk in Los Angeles. Avery assembled some used machine parts to create and patent the first self-adhesive, die-cut labelling machine. The device would come to be known as a 'price gun' because of its appearance and the manner in which it allowed users to rapidly affix pricing labels to individual products.

Shortly after developing his innovative product, Avery created a company to produce self-adhesive labels, which he began supplying to the Dennison Manufacturing Company. After more than half a century of working together, the two firms merged to form Avery Dennison in 1990.

By the time of their merger, the price gun was seldom seen in retail operations. Its usage had been greatly diminished by the development of the barcode and point-of-sale scanning systems. The barcode eliminated retailers' need to apply price labels to individual items in all but a handful of special situations where regulations required continued use of the practice as a form of consumer protection, designed to ensure accuracy with shelf edge prices.

Contribution to Retail History

The development of the price gun was a major technological step forward for the retail industry. It simplified operations for retailers of fast-turning consumer packaged goods and instilled trust in shoppers by improving price transparency and accuracy. Although seldom used today, the price gun's development impacted retail efficiency and enabled retailers to establish a new store experience for their shoppers.

Shopping Trolley

IN 1936, SYLVAN NATHAN GOLDMAN, AN ENTREPRENEUR AND STORE OWNER FROM OKLAHOMA, REALISED THAT RETAIL PURCHASES WERE RESTRICTED TO WHAT THE SHOPPER COULD CARRY HOME. WORKING WITH MECHANIC, FRED YOUNG, TOGETHER THEY CREATED A SHOPPING TROLLEY.

MADE WITH A METAL FRAME IT HAD TWO WIRE BASKETS. CUSTOMERS COULD PLACE THEIR HAND-HELD BASKETS ON THE CARRIERS AND TAKE THEM OFF AGAIN AT THE CHECKOUT. THE TROLLEYS BECAME KNOWN AS 'FOLDING BASKET CARRIER CARTS' AND GOLDMAN SET UP A COMPANY TO PRODUCE THEM CALLED THE 'FOLDING CARRIER BASKET COMPANY'.

A patent war followed in 1946, when Orla Watson of Kansas City, wanted to produce a telescoping trolley, but Goldman filed for a similar patent. In 1949, Goldman gave his patent rights and royalties to Watson but kept the 'licensing rights' for himself. By 1947, shopping trolleys had child seats and by 1954, coloured handles and personalised store names.

However, Goldman's trolleys did not have an easy reception from customers in the early days. Young women thought the trolleys unfashionable and young men thought they would appear weak if they used a trolley. Then came the marketing campaign. Goldman hired models of all ages and both sexes to push the trolleys around the store, pretending they were shopping. Attractive store greeters met the shoppers as they came in and encouraged them to use their carts. Trolleys increased sales for all stores that adopted them, as shoppers were better able to self-serve throughout the store and make more purchases.

Contribution to Retail History

Customers were no longer restricted to buying the amount of goods they could carry in a basket. This, and being able to wander the streets in comfort, encouraged them to buy more. The success of the trolley is also closely associated with the rise in car ownership, as bulk buying was only possible if the customer had access to a car to transport the goods home. Like the advent of refrigeration, the trolley was partly responsible for the transition to less frequent supermarket shopping occasions as customers could do a weekly shop. The supermarket itself was redesigned to accommodate the trolleys, including wider aisles and new checkout counters.

'High Street'

'HIGH STREET' WAS FIRST PUBLISHED IN 1938. IT SHOWCASED 24 COLOUR LITHOGRAPHS BY THE ILLUSTRATOR, ERIC RAVILIOUS, WITH ACCOMPANYING TEXT BY THE ARCHITECTURAL HISTORIAN, J.M. RICHARDS.

Ravilious created his lithographs in 1936 and 1937, drawing straight onto stone in the studios of the Curwen Press. The idea of an alphabet of shops came from his lover, Helen Binyon. The book was actually designed for children. The Ravilious images evoke nostalgia for a past era of shopping, but in the case of the cheesemonger (Paxton & Whitfield in Jermyn Street) the shop façade and window display still remain much the same today.

Initially, Ravilious did not have a publisher, but continued working on the book, subsidised by Curwen Press until Noel Carrington (brother of the Bloomsbury artist, Dora Carrington) agreed to publish it. Sadly, only 2,000 copies of 'High Street' were printed and the lithographic plates were subsequently destroyed by the London Blitz. Today, it is an extremely collectable item, and copies change hands at high prices.

Contribution to Retail History

'High Street' captures a bygone era in retail, just before the face of the UK High Street began to change. In the 1930s, retail brands such as Marks & Spencer, Boots and Woolworth's began to expand their national presence, taking up positions in the High Street and replacing the small, individual shopkeepers depicted in this book.

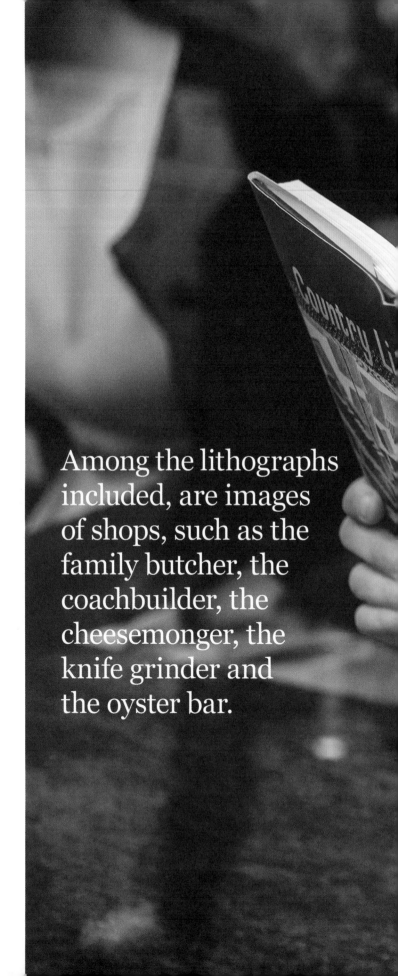

Among the lithographs included, are images of shops, such as the family butcher, the coachbuilder, the cheesemonger, the knife grinder and the oyster bar.

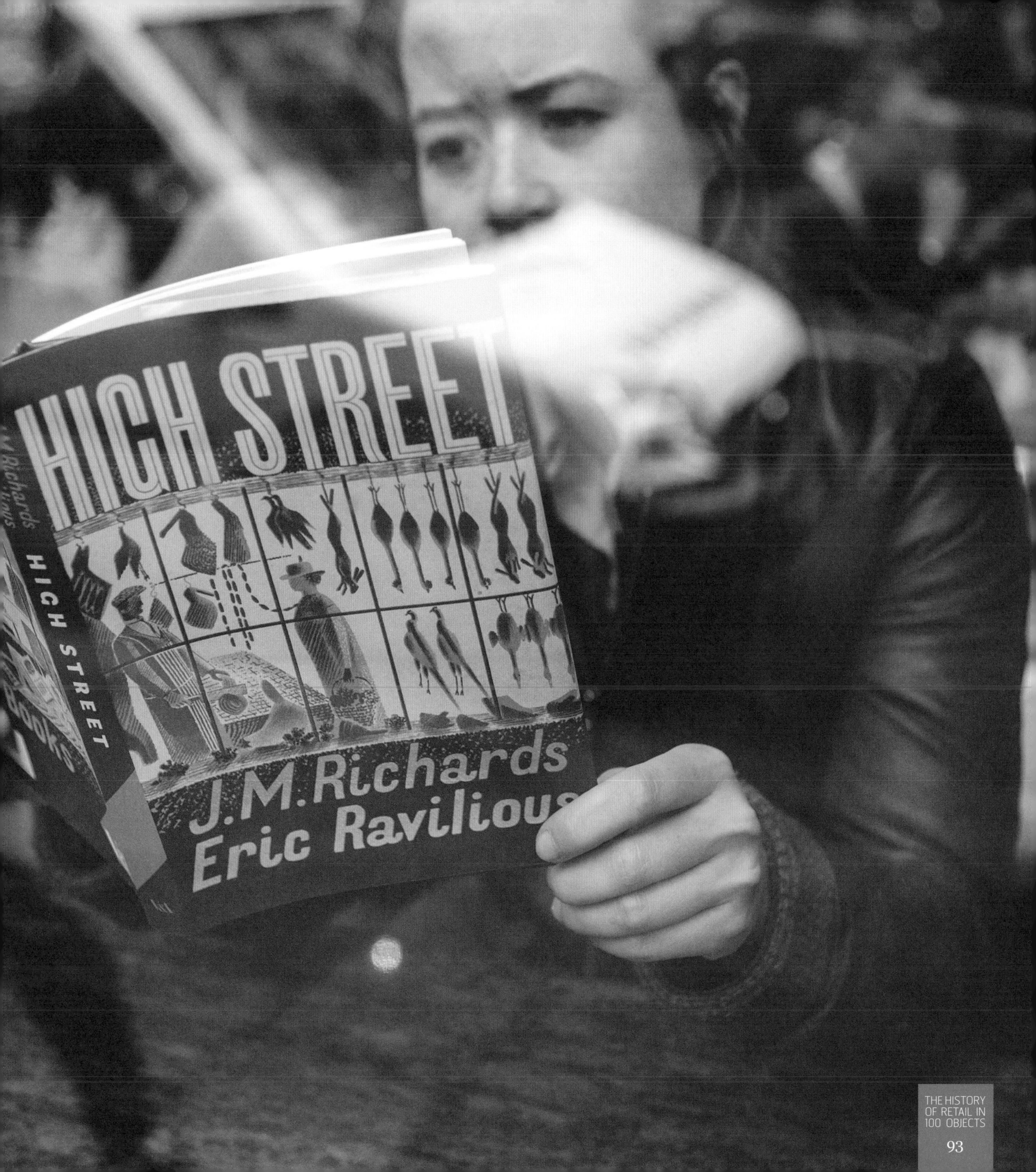
HIGH STREET
J.M.Richards
Eric Ravilious
HIGH STREET

Fluorescent Tube

PRIOR TO THE DEVELOPMENT OF THE FLUORESCENT TUBE (OFTEN REFERRED TO AS 'STRIP LIGHTING'), RETAILERS WERE RELIANT ON THE STANDARD 'INCANDESCENT' LIGHT BULB.

THE ARRIVAL OF FLUORESCENT LIGHTING GAVE THEM A HIGHLY ECONOMICAL ALTERNATIVE. FLUORESCENT LIGHTS PRODUCE A LOT OF LIGHT – IDEAL FOR ILLUMINATING MERCHANDISE TO ITS BEST ADVANTAGE, DAY OR NIGHT – CONSUME VERY LITTLE ENERGY, AND GENERATE VERY LITTLE HEAT. THE AVERAGE LIFE OF FLUORESCENT BULBS IS LONG, REDUCING THE LABOUR INVOLVED IN REPLACING THEM.

Think of a light bulb and you summon up the name of Thomas Edison, its inventor, but although Edison dabbled with fluorescent lighting, he lost interest in it. Others experimented further, but it wasn't until 1901 that Peter Cooper Hewitt patented the first 'mercury vapour lamp', which was the prototype of the fluorescent tube.

Hewitt's work built on that of German physicist, Julius Plucker, and glassblower, Heinrich Geissler, who realised that if you passed an electric current through a glass tube with small amounts of gas in it, you could make light. Hewitt began experimenting and discovered that the brightness of these mercury-filled lights was truly illuminating. The lights would be too bright for domestic homes, so his thoughts turned to photographic use and industrial studios. Together with George Westinghouse, he formed the Cooper Hewitt Electric Company to produce the first commercial mercury lamps. In 1934, Edmund Germer, whose lights were more powerful and better suited to smaller spaces, adapted their concept.

In 1936, George Inman of General Electric (GE) in Ohio, filed for a patent and GE began to prepare to introduce these lamps commercially. On April 21, 1938, the company's fluorescent MAZDA lamps were put on sale. They produced 'coloured lights' and offered economies and efficiencies that would forever change lighting in retail stores.

Contribution to Retail History

The fluorescent tube allowed retailers to illuminate their stores more economically, while generating less heat and facilitated extended opening hours. Lighting could also now be used to create different ambiences throughout different parts of the store – the concept of 'mood lighting'. It also had a positive impact on merchandising displays, enabling lighting within fixtures, not purely from an overhead source.

Ration Book

DURING THE 1930s, 40s, AND EVEN INTO THE 1950s, RATIONING CHANGED THE FACE OR RETAILING IN THE UK. BRITISH CITIZENS WERE NO LONGER LIVING IN AN AGE OF PLENTY, SCARCITY BECAME THE NORM.

THE UK RATION BOOK CONTAINED COUPONS THAT CUSTOMERS TRADED IN AT THE SHOP, AND THE SHOPKEEPER SENT THEM TO THE MINISTRY TO BE COUNTED. EVEN THE BRITISH ROYAL FAMILY HAD RATION BOOKS.

The UK's Ministry of Food decided what a person's basic needs were and set a weekly allowance accordingly. Tea, cheese, butter, margarine, bacon, porridge, wheat flakes, shredded wheat, lard, sugar and eggs were all rationed. Customers were limited by what the store had been supplied with. There was little choice and availability of goods might vary from week to week.

An adult was allowed one egg per week, 2oz. of bacon, 2oz. of margarine and 2oz. of tea. Lemons and bananas became very scarce and while oranges continued to be sold, greengrocers used to reserve them for children and pregnant women, who had special rationing books. Bread was not rationed, nor was fish, but fish prices were controlled. Biscuits were measured out loose and sweets were rationed to 4oz. per week per person.

Prices were fixed by the Ministry of Food. Jam, bread and milk would cost the same whatever store you went to. This system – RPM (Retail Price Maintenance)

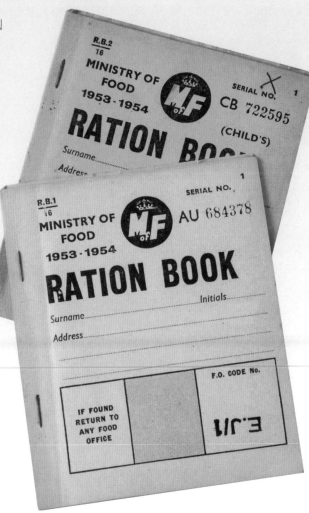

continued for some goods until the 1960s. Clothes were rationed too, on a points system. Petrol was sold only for work and a permit was needed to obtain it.

In May 1942, an order was passed that meals served in UK hotels and restaurants must not cost more than five shillings per customer, and must not be more than three courses. In the same year, the Board of Trade laid down a Civilian Clothing Order to regulate the manufacture and distribution of clothing.

By rationing, the Ministry of Food achieved their aim of ensuring supplies lasted and there was enough to go round – just.

Rationing of food ended on July 4, 1954, 14 years after it began.

Contribution to Retail History

Rationing meant UK retailers had to sell the same goods at the same price, restricting competition and putting the brakes firmly on all the advancements that might otherwise have arisen. The lifting of rationing acted as a catalyst for innovation as UK retailers could again look forward to growth.

Pallet

IT'S EASY TO TAKE FOR GRANTED THE RETAIL PROGRESS THAT QUITE MUNDANE OBJECTS HAVE INITIATED. THE PALLET IS A TYPICAL EXAMPLE. WOODEN PALLETS, PLASTIC PALLETS, METAL PALLETS — ALL ALLOW GOODS TO BE STACKED AND STORED ON THEM, TO BE LIFTED AND MOVED AROUND WITH RELATIVE EASE.

PALLETS ARE STRONG; THEY CAN CARRY LOADS OF 1,000 KG, AND AS MORE GOODS ARE TRANSPORTED VIA CONTAINER TRUCKS AND SHIPS, THE PALLET INDUSTRY HAS BURGEONED.

An amazing half a billion pallets are made each year, with around two billion pallets apparently in use across the US alone. Once merchandise is stored on a pallet, it can be lifted by forklift trucks or by equipment called 'pallet jacks'. Warehouse layouts are designed to enable the forklifts to weave in and out of the storage shelves that hold the pallets on them. Large discount stores and 'sheds' (for example DIY retail outlets) use pallets to store and display merchandise within the retail environment itself.

The use of pallets reduces retailers' handling and storage costs by allowing ease of movement. Surprisingly, there is no single international standard for pallet sizes, but in principle, those pallets used in shipping have to be made of materials that won't carry insects or plant diseases.

Contribution to Retail History

Unassumingly modest, the humble pallet has become fundamental to the smooth running of the supply chain. A vital merchandising tool for retailers like Aldi, Costco and Walmart, the pallet is used as an efficient display by retailers across the world. Globally, trillions of dollars worth of merchandise is sold from pallets.

www.retail100objects.com

Speciality Store

SPECIALITY STORES ARE READILY IDENTIFIED BY THEIR FOCUS ON SPECIFIC MERCHANDISE CLASSIFICATIONS OR MULTIPLE PRODUCT RANGES OFFERED UNDER A SINGLE BRAND.

SPECIALITY STORES TAP INTO SHOPPERS' DESIRE FOR INCREASED CHOICE WITHIN SELECT CATEGORIES OR BRANDS AND THEY GIVE THE MODERN RETAIL INDUSTRY ITS APPEARANCE OF SEEMINGLY LIMITLESS OFFERINGS.

The speciality store stands in sharp contrast to the typical discount or department store where the appeal to shoppers is based on a broad selection of merchandise with limited range within categories. Conversely, speciality stores created a new value proposition for shoppers that was based on the depth of product assortment within specific categories or brands. The new approach to retailing gained broad acceptance following the Second World War. Retailers recognised that increased consumer demand had created the opportunity to appeal to ever narrower segments of the market with stores that offered specialised merchandise assortment or specific brands. Shoppers found the depth of assortment presented by the speciality store very alluring and their spending behaviours gave rise to the speciality store movement of the last half century.

The earliest speciality stores tended to focus on large product categories such as shoes, sporting goods, jewellery or menswear. However, as the speciality store segment of the retail industry evolved, the merchandise classifications became increasingly narrow. Speciality stores now exist for specific types and brands of shoes within the footwear category and the same is true for a category such as sporting goods where speciality

stores exist for the fly-fishing segment of the fishing category within sporting goods.

The trend of increased specialisation within the speciality store retail segment gained new momentum with the dawn of e-commerce in the late 1990s. Online shopping suddenly made it possible for speciality store operators to take the principles of serving shoppers with an extensive product offering across a narrow range of categories to an unprecedented and more finely segmented level. Unbound by the constraints of physical stores the speciality store stands as an even more significant force in a digital world where shopper choice is unconstrained by the limitations of physical stores.

Contribution to Retail History

The speciality store represented a new approach to serving shoppers and created powerful growth opportunities for retailers and brands. By offering deep product assortments within narrow merchandise classifications, retailers created a new approach that had powerful appeal in a marketplace with shoppers who were receptive to the greater level of choice that speciality stores afforded.

Tupperware

IN 1946, EARL SILAS TUPPER DEVELOPED A NEW FORM OF HOME STORAGE CONTAINERS. MADE OF PLASTIC, WITH WHAT WAS KNOWN AS A 'BURPING SEAL', THESE CONTAINERS WERE AIRTIGHT AND IDEAL FOR FOOD STORAGE.

Contribution to Retail History

The Tupperware marketing and distribution model was enormously successful and is still applied globally today. Largely attributable to Brownie Wise's ability to create marketing strategies that tapped into popular culture and encouraged women to sign up to become hosts, her belief that "if we build the people, they'll build the business" created a new retail paradigm.

THE PRODUCTS WERE A GREAT DEVELOPMENT IN THEMSELVES, BUT IT WAS THE PIONEERING APPROACH TO SALES AND MARKETING OF TUPPERWARE THAT MADE ITS MARK ON RETAIL HISTORY.

Led by Brownie Wise, formerly a sales representative for Stanley Home Products, Tupper began to promote his product via the 'party plan' approach. The concept of home selling had been around since the 1920s but the 'Tupperware Party' became the first internationally recognised scheme of its kind. A simple idea, American housewives were recruited to host a Tupperware Party in their homes, to which they invited friends and neighbours to see and buy the Tupperware product line. The hosts were incentivised with free products and a 'prize', the size of which depended on their sales figures. Being able to demonstrate the product features within the home environment helped to gain women's trust and encouraged them to purchase.

Women could work themselves up from host to manager and ultimately to the position of distributor. This was at a time when women, who had grown accustomed to working and earning during the Second World War, were being encouraged to "go back to the kitchen" in order to free up paid positions for men. The opportunity to earn some independent income while still being able to run the home ensured widespread take up of the scheme by women across the US – and massive sales success for Tupperware.

Closed Circuit Television

THE ORIGINS OF CLOSED CIRCUIT TELEVISION CAN BE TRACED TO THE SECOND WORLD WAR WHEN GERMANY USED THE TECHNOLOGY IN THE DEVELOPMENT OF V-2 ROCKETS.

DESPITE AN INAUSPICIOUS BEGINNING, CLOSED CIRCUIT TELEVISION WOULD GO ON TO PLAY AN IMPORTANT ROLE IN THE RETAIL INDUSTRY.

Commonly referred to as CCTV, the system of video cameras connected to display monitors and recording devices, enabled Germany to monitor rocket launches from a closer distance than had previously been possible. CCTV would go on to have a much broader application in countless industries that recognised the value of capturing, displaying and storing video information. Many of the earliest applications were related to security and asset protection purposes in industries such are retail, casinos, financial services, correctional facilities and government institutions.

Retailers in particular placed CCTV cameras in strategic and discrete locations to detect the actions and to aid in the prosecution of those engaged in various types of wrongdoing. Meanwhile, retailers leveraged the deterrence capabilities of CCTV systems by placing cameras in high visibility locations.

The effectiveness of CCTV for asset protection purposes resulted in widespread usage. More recently, technological developments and reduced costs have led to the development of new capabilities. Retailers are leveraging the video streams generated by CCTV systems to yield new sources of shopper insights. Ongoing advancements in resolution and lens size now allow for shelf edge camera placement, which enables retailers to determine shoppers' approximate age, gender and ethnicity to optimise sales strategies and generate heat maps of customer traffic based on dwell times in specific locations.

Contribution to Retail History

CCTV's impact on the retail industry was dramatic because it allowed operators to increase the security of their stores and parking lots, while enhancing the sales potential of theft-prone products which could be more openly merchandised with a reduced risk of loss. Shopper insights generated by CCTV systems allowed retailers to better understand customer traffic, optimise store layouts and operate more efficiently.

Discount Store

DISCOUNT STORES OFFERED A WIDE RANGE OF MERCHANDISE CATEGORIES AND EMPLOYED A PRICING PHILOSOPHY THAT PROVED SO POPULAR WITH SHOPPERS IT WOULD COME TO DOMINATE THE INDUSTRY.

The earliest discount stores sought to satisfy shoppers' everyday needs for a wide range of basic products, as well as, an assortment of discretionary items. The discount pricing philosophy required operators to be mindful of capital costs and operating expenses so as to generate an acceptable level of profitability by selling products at lower prices. This resulted in a more austere shopping experience than what customers were accustomed to at traditional department stores of the day, but the 'no frills' approach presented by the likes of Aldi and Lidl was a trade-off many were willing to make in exchange for significant savings.

Today, the stores operated by traditional discount retailers such as Walmart, Kmart and Target, bear little resemblance to the store formats of the 1960s and 1970s which propelled them to dominance in American retailing. The addition of food to their traditional product offerings has transformed many locations into large supermarkets while retailers, such as Dollar General and Family Dollar have emerged as a new breed of discount store.

Contribution to Retail History

Discount stores and the pricing philosophy which underpins the concept, changed the retail industry by altering shoppers' perceptions of value. Price became the overriding consideration for many shoppers to the point where many retailers who operated formats other than traditional discount stores had at the core of their value proposition, a discount pricing philosophy.

www.retail100objects.com

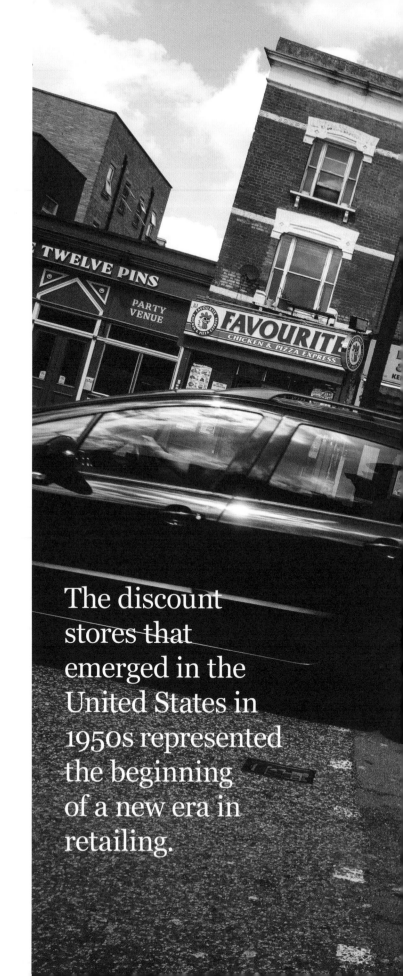

The discount stores that emerged in the United States in 1950s represented the beginning of a new era in retailing.

Computer

IT WAS THE BRITISH RESTAURANT, FOOD, HOTEL AND TEASHOP CHAIN, J LYONS & CO., WHO FIRST SAW THE POTENTIAL FOR USE OF THE COMPUTER IN RETAIL.

BETWEEN 1947 AND 1963, THE COMPANY MANUFACTURED AND SOLD A RANGE OF LEO (LYONS ELECTRONIC OFFICE) COMPUTERS. THIS DEVELOPMENT WAS HAPPENING FAR AHEAD OF SIMILAR EFFORTS IN AMERICA OR ELSEWHERE.

The LEO computer, built in 1951, was designed by Dr John Pilkerton and John Simmons to handle the company's accounts and logistics. In 1963, the LEO business merged with English Electric's computer interests to form the English Electric LEO.

Before computers entered retail, the store manager was in charge of manually arranging the purchasing and selling the merchandise. He would decide what items to keep in stock, how much they should sell for, who to employ, and how much to pay them.

In the 1960s, computers in retail began to be used to manage customer data and expedite accounting processes, just as the Lyons group had done in the first instance. Credit cards were beginning to be used more frequently, and cash registers and calculators were also speeding up the checkout process for customers.

Walmart, and other discount stores such as Kmart and Target, were early adopters of computer technology and by the mid-1980s and early 1990s small shops had computers.

They all used 'inventory control computing' systems to keep track of what goods the store had and to let them know when items should be restocked. Computer software systems also helped manage the employee payrolls and day-to-day accounts. The turnaround time for stocking systems improved significantly and more customers were processed through checkouts, more swiftly.

By 1993, Walmart computer systems had satellite links, allowing stores to send orders to suppliers by these satellite links.

Contribution to Retail History

As the basis of success for many retailers, the computer became the beating heart at the centre of functions such as buying, supply chain, replenishment, merchandising, HR and more. Arguably, the effective use of computing was behind the rise to global supremacy for retailers such as Amazon and Walmart. Ironically, the computer has now become the store of the future and threatens the survival of many traditional retailers.

Credit Card

IN 1946 A NEW YORK BANKER, JOHN BIGGINS, INTRODUCED HIS 'CHARGE-IT' CARD. WHEN THIS CARD WAS USED TO BUY GOODS FROM A SHOP, THE SALES SLIP WAS SENT ON TO BIGGINS'S BANK. THE BANK THEN PAID THE MONEY TO THE MERCHANTS AND GOT THEIR CUSTOMERS TO PAY THEM IN RETURN.

IN 1951 FRANKLIN NATIONAL BANK IN NEW YORK ISSUED ITS FIRST BANK CREDIT CARD, WHICH COULD ONLY BE USED BY THAT BANK'S ACCOUNT HOLDERS. AT THE SAME TIME, FRANK MCNAMARA WAS DEVELOPING THE DINERS CLUB CARD.

In 1949, McNamara dined in New York's Major's Cabin Grill, and when the bill arrived, realised he had left his wallet behind. Deciding an alternative to cash was needed, he came up with the Diners Club Card, used mainly for entertaining and travel. For this reason, the Diners Card is recognised as being the first credit card in general use.

It was not until 1958 that American Express launched its first credit card, made from cardboard or celluloid. A year later production switched to using plastic. Momentum built and American Express launched local currency cards in other countries. Within five years, approximately 1 million cards were in use, accepted at about 85,000 establishments in the USA and elsewhere.

In 1959, MasterCard claims to have been the first to introduce a new concept which allowed customers to 'roll' their balance over so they didn't have to pay it all off at the end of a set cycle of payment. 1966 saw the move to 'general purpose cards' when the Bank of America franchised its BankAmericard brand — that we now know as Visa — to banks nationwide. Also at this time, a group of banks were working together to create the InterBank Card Association, known now as MasterCard — a direct competitor with Visa.

Contribution to Retail History

The proliferation of credit cards encouraged a 'buy now, pay later' consumer mind-set and so powered more retail spending. With the advent of online shopping, the credit card has become the default form of payment that has fuelled the growth of e-commerce transactions, even if they do not choose to take up the 'credit' element but settle the full amount monthly.

Shannon Airport

IN MARCH 1947, THE IRISH PARLIAMENT PASSED LEGISLATION THAT HERALDED THE ARRIVAL OF THE GLOBAL DUTY FREE INDUSTRY.

THE 'CUSTOMS FREE ACT' MEANT THAT NORMAL DUTY AND TAX PROCEDURES DID NOT APPLY TO PASSENGERS PURCHASING GOODS AT SHANNON AIRPORT.

This radical retail development was largely down to the efforts and entrepreneurialism of one man, Brendan O'Regan. He had been the Catering Comptroller at Foynes, which was the refuelling point for seaplanes between the UK and US. In 1945, O'Regan was transferred to the airbase at Shannon and it was here that he identified the opportunity to offer goods for sale to transit passengers. However, he took his idea further, managing to persuade the airport authorities that the transit area was not part of the Irish state and therefore goods purchased within it should not be liable for taxes and duties.

Having gained the support of Parliament and seen the legislation passed, in May 1947, O'Regan opened the world's first Duty Free shop, staffed by one woman, Ms Kitty Downes. Offering a service for Trans-Atlantic airline passengers typically travelling between Europe and North America whose flights stopped for refuelling on both outbound and inbound journeys, it was an immediate success.

To begin with, the Duty Free shop was a small kiosk in Shannon Airport's terminal building and it predominantly sold souvenirs. However, because of the duty free savings, goods were often cheaper than in the country of manufacture, making luxury goods affordable to travellers for the first time. The reputation of Duty Free quickly spread and the product lines expanded to encompass quality international branded merchandise, including brands such as Rosenthal porcelain and Leica cameras.

In 1951, Shannon Airport scored another first with the opening of the first Airport Duty Free Liquor Shop. It began as a ship's store where airline stewards purchased supplies for re-sale to passengers when the aircraft became airborne. Soon, passengers were allowed to make direct purchases at tax-free prices, albeit on a restricted basis. In the beginning, Shannon Duty Free applied only to liquor and tobacco, but it rapidly spread to encompass the vast range of Duty Free departments familiar to the modern international traveller.

In the 1950s, Duty Free shopping spread to the US and in 1960 two Americans, Charles Feeney and Robert Miller, started Duty Free Shops (now DFS). DFS began by operating in Hong Kong and rapidly expanded globally. By the mid-1990s, Duty Free shopping had spread to overland, sea and air travel in more than 80 different countries.

Contribution to Retail History

Shannon Airport's Duty Free shop was groundbreaking in that it created a new retail channel and led to the development of a different kind of shopping environment, soon replicated at air and seaports across the globe. Retail concessions within airports have contributed enormously to airport authority revenues and helped drive expansion. The concessions have been able to capitalise on a captive audience. In the early days, unaffordable luxury brands, being sold free of tax and duty were put within the reach of a new audience: the international traveller, further enhancing the cachet of those brands.

Tetra Pak

TETRA PAK IS BASED ON 'ASEPTIC PACKAGING TECHNOLOGY' THAT ALLOWS PERISHABLE PRODUCTS TO BE KEPT COLD AND FRESH THROUGHOUT THE DISTRIBUTION AND STORAGE CHAIN.

THE INSTITUTE OF FOOD TECHNOLOGISTS CONSIDERS ITS DEVELOPMENT TO BE THE MOST IMPORTANT FOOD PACKAGING INNOVATION OF THE 20TH CENTURY.

The process allows the product and the package to be sterilised separately, then combined and sealed in a sterile atmosphere (whereas in canning processes, the product and the package are combined and then sterilised). UHT − ultra-heat treated foodstuffs such as milk, juice, and processed foods such as vegetables and fruit, when sealed in aseptic packaging can be stored at room temperature for up to a year.

The Swedish Company that created Tetra Pak is now the largest food packaging company in the world by sales. How did it begin? At the end of the 1920s, Ruben Rausing was the owner of a food carton company in Malmo. He had seen self-service grocery stores in America and recognised that pre-packaged foods (a better and more hygienic way of handling foods) were part of retail's future.

Rausing wanted to pre-package liquids too, and invested heavily in research and development work to do so. In 1944, the company's lab came up with the idea of making a tetrahedron shaped package out of a tube of paper. Rausing filed for a patent on 27th March 1944, but work continued for the rest of the decade, solving the problems of

how to fill, store and distribute liquids in this way. It was Rausing's wife, Elisabeth, who suggested continuously sealing the package, as if stuffing sausages, to prevent oxygen getting in. Working with Swedish paper mills and foreign chemical companies, a paper coated with polythene was produced. This made the paper waterproof and it could also be heatsealed.

AB Tetra Pak was set up in Lund, Sweden in 1951 and the new packaging system was presented to the press. In 1952, the first filling machine, which was able to package 100ml cream tetrahedrons, was delivered to a local dairy.

Contribution to Retail History

Tetra Pak's aseptic packaging technology enabled the packaging and distribution of a much wider range of foodstuffs than ever before. As well as its enhanced storage attributes, it is also lightweight and can be manufactured in uniform shapes, helping make the distribution and retailing process more efficient and cost-effective. Products that have previously not been big sellers (due to the difficulties of keeping them fresh) have been able to expand their distribution footprint.

THE BARCODE'S RETAIL HISTORY BEGAN IN 1952 WHEN THE FIRST PATENT FOR A BARCODE TYPE PRODUCT WAS ISSUED TO INVENTORS JOSEPH WOODLAND AND BERNARD SILVER.

Barcode

BUT IT WAS AN INVENTION AHEAD OF ITS TIME AND IT TOOK ANOTHER 22 YEARS FOR THE FIRST PRODUCT WITH A BARCODE TO BE SOLD IN A SHOP.

Silver and Woodland were graduate students at Drexel Institute of Technology in Philadelphia. A local food chain asked the Institute if it could research a method of automatically reading product information during checkout. Woodland's first design used patterns of ink that glowed under ultraviolet light, but the ink was unstable and expensive. Undefeated, Woodland quit his teaching job at Drexel, took some stock market earnings and moved to Florida to work on the problem.

Trial and error resulted in the development of a 'straight line pattern'. It had four white lines on a dark background. The information was coded by the presence or absence of one or more of the lines. Eureka!

Neither Woodland nor Silver made much money from their invention and they sold the patent to RCA (The Radio Corporation of America) for a relatively small sum of money. The RCA code had problems and it was left to Logicon, Inc, to work with The National Association of Food Chains, to develop an industry-wide barcode system. By 1970, an industry standard had developed – the Universal Grocery Products Identification Code or UGPIC.

The first product to have a barcode was a packet of Wrigley's chewing gum. On June 26, 1974 at 8:01 a.m., Sharon Buchana, a checker at Marsh's Supermarket in Troy, Ohio, scanned the 10-pack of Wrigley's Juicy Fruit chewing gum. It cost 67 cents. It was the first item lifted out of the shopping cart by a shopper, Clyde Dawson. Today, that pack of gum is on display at the Smithsonian Institution's National Museum of American History.

Contribution to Retail History

The barcode was a retail revolution. It improved the speed and accuracy of the checkout process, enabled better stock management and planning for retailers and facilitated end-to-end supply chain automation. The fabric of modern retailing is built on the foundations of the humble barcode. Nothing else so small has had such a profound impact.

Forklift Truck

SUPERMARKETS, BIG CHAIN STORES AND SMALL STORES ALIKE, ALL RELY ON STORING VAST QUANTITIES OF GOODS IN WAREHOUSE AND DISTRIBUTION CENTRES ACROSS THEIR SUPPLY CHAIN, READY TO BE TRANSFERRED TO TRUCKS AND DRIVEN THROUGH THE NIGHT TO GET TO YOUR LOCAL BRANCH OF THEIR STORE.

Forklift trucks were specially designed to navigate the wide aisles of the distribution centres, taking the pallets off the shelves onto waiting lorries.

Early civilisations have always used a 'lever' of some kind for lifting and in the 19th century, manually powered sack trucks were in common use. The modern forklift was developed in the 1960s by a number of companies, bringing together mechanical advancements in the US, the UK and Japan.

In 1906, the Pennsylvania Railroad in the US had battery powered platform trucks for moving luggage, and in the UK, the Ipswich-based engineering company, Ransomes, Sims and Jeffries used various types of material handling equipment to overcome labour shortages during the First World War. In 1917 in the US, Clark started using powered lift tractors in their factories and in 1919, Towmotor Company. In 1920 Yale & Towne Manufacturing also began producing forklift trucks. One of the impacts of the two world wars was improved use of the forklift technology and warehousing, as huge quantities of cargo were loaded onto ships and containers bound for the troops.

Today, warehouse forklifts can lift loads between one to five tonnes, while shipping forklifts can lift up to 50 tonnes.

Contribution to Retail History

The invention of the forklift (and its work partner, the pallet) allowed suppliers and retailers to move products more effectively throughout the supply chain. Without the forklift, global giants like Costco and Metro would have struggled to achieve the scale, scope and profitability of the operations they enjoy today.

Southdale Center

SOUTHDALE IN EDINA, MINNEAPOLIS, MINNESOTA, OPENED IN 1956. IT WAS THE WORLD'S FIRST FULLY ENCLOSED, CLIMATE CONTROLLED MALL.

MUCH EXPANDED AND EXTENDED OVER THE INTERVENING YEARS, IT NOW HOUSES 120 SPECIALITY STORES, RESTAURANTS, BARS AND A CINEMA.

Southdale, also known as 'Southdale Center', was developed by the Dayton Company, who owned Dayton's department store in Minneapolis. It cost $20 million dollars to build. Designed by Victor Gruen, (an Austrian immigrant), it was modelled on the malls and arcades of European cities. Gruen disliked the suburban lifestyle of 1950s America and set about designing a building that would bring people together in a place with a sense of community. He wanted to achieve an atmosphere of leisure and excitement, as well as, intimacy and to this end he incorporated paintings, decorative lighting, fountains, tropical plants and flowers in his design.

The Southdale Center housed a branch of Dayton's, Donaldson's, Walgreens Pharmacy, Woolworth's and many other large retail brands. Its opening day attracted 40,000 visitors – a feat that proved that this new retail model was destined to be a great success.

Contribution to Retail History

Southdale was designed with two things in mind, the consumer and the future. Its creators recognised that consumers were increasingly looking for convenience and variety and so the mall was designed to be a one-stop destination housing a wide variety of retail outlets, services and leisure activities. It became a blueprint for similar malls across the developed world.

Shipping Container

SINCE THE 1950s, STEEL SHIPPING CONTAINERS HAVE BEEN USED MAINLY FOR INTERNATIONAL OCEAN SHIPPING – BUT THEY ARE ALSO USED FOR TRUCK AND TRAIN FREIGHT, AND SOMETIMES STORAGE TOO.

MOST ARE ABOUT 40 BY 20 FEET, AND THE TERM TEW (MEANING 20 FOOT CONTAINER) IS USED WHEN DESCRIBING THEM, WITH 2 TEW REFERRING TO A 40-FOOT CONTAINER.

Standardised containers speeded up the packing process and allowed more efficient loading and unloading techniques to take place from trucks to ships and warehouses. A secure, stable storage receptacle, they can also be boxed to be stacked onto another, up to ten high.

The first shipping container was patented in 1956 by Malcolm McLean, an American trucker from North Carolina, working with engineer Keith Tantlinger. McLean brought his first truck in 1934 and by 1956 owned the largest trucking fleet in the South – the fifth largest in the US.

He took over the Pan Atlantic (Steamship) Tanker Company, which owned some old tankers. He renamed his company Sea-Land Shipping, and after further development work, designed a shipping container that could be lifted directly from a vehicle onto a ship, without first having to load and reload the content.

This shipping container was a uniform size, strong, theft-resistant, stackable, easy to load and could be used on roads, rail, ship and truck. The stacking system was called 'intermodalism'. A revolution in cargo transportation had begun. The speed at which cargo could now be loaded, reduced costs by more than 90% and because the containers were robust, the goods arrived at their destination in better condition.

Contribution to Retail History

Standardised shipping containers led to faster, more efficient loading and enabled a massive growth in international trading and the creation of lean supply chain possibilities. More cost-effective, safer loading and transportation, encouraged more mass production and distribution overseas. The increased efficiencies, greater security and reductions in damage and theft lowered the supply chain costs, enabling cheaper prices in stores. Refrigerated containers allowed the transportation of perishable goods across vast distances.

Bubble Wrap

The story of plastic transparent Bubble Wrap begins in 1957 with two inventors and engineers: Al Fielding and Marc Chavannes, from New Jersey, USA. They originally set out to produce a textured wallpaper.

The pair began by sealing two shower curtains together, which in the process would capture air bubbles that they envisaged would give their wallpaper a textured feel. However, the wallpaper idea failed to gain any traction so they looked for an alternative use for their new product. Their thoughts turned to greenhouse insulation but again, the idea did not take off.

Into the frame stepped Frederick W. Bowers, a marketer at the Sealed Air Company, which just so happened to be co-founded by Fielding. Bowers realised that the new 1401 computers which IBM had just launched could benefit from using Bubble Wrap to protect them in shipping. He pitched the idea to IBM and showed them the protective qualities of Bubble Wrap. IBM embraced the product and used it to transport their new 1401 computers and other fragile products all over the world. By the mid-1960s about half of all the computers in the world were the IBM 1401, many of which would not have arrived at their destination in one piece without Bubble Wrap.

It's said that each year Sealed Air produces enough Bubble Wrap to wrap around the Earth's equator, about ten times. It's estimated that around $400 million of Bubble Wrap is sold annually. Simple though the product is, it has moved with the times to the extent that there is a new 'DIY-inflatable Bubble Wrap'. Customers buy the product flat and lease a special machine from Sealed Air to inflate it, thereby reducing the costs of transportation for the manufacturers of products.

Today Bubble Wrap is most commonly used for food packaging but it is also widely used by householders to protect fragile possessions in house moves or in the post – and of course, for popping as a pastime.

Contribution to Retail History

Bubble Wrap has helped bolster the popularity of mail order and online shopping as retailers and consumers alike have confidence in its power to protect merchandise on its journey from one place to the other. Less damage and breakage also reduces the costs of returns to the retailer.

Cash and Carry

THE CASH AND CARRY FORM OF RETAILING EMERGED IN THE MID-1900s AS CUSTOMERS OF TRADITIONAL WHOLESALERS WERE OFFERED A NEW APPROACH TO PURCHASING MERCHANDISE.

THE PROCESS OF SELF-SELECTING MERCHANDISE FROM A WAREHOUSE OR SHOWROOM ENVIRONMENT, RENDERING PAYMENT ON THE SPOT AND TRANSPORTING MERCHANDISE, RESULTED IN A FORM OF RETAILING THAT CAME TO BE KNOWN AS CASH AND CARRY.

Lawrence Batley of Huddersfield, England is credited with inventing the cash and carry philosophy and successfully applying it to a retail enterprise. He opened Batley's Cash and Carry in 1958 and inspired a number of competitors to launch similar concepts.

The retail concept was born out of a recognition that shoppers were willing to forego some of the conveniences offered by traditional wholesalers such as delivery and extended payment terms. Cash and carry offered shoppers a different type of value proposition that emphasised low prices, the opportunity to discover new products in a warehouse shopping environment and the convenience of taking immediate possession of purchases. The combination proved appealing to businesses who formed the core customer base of traditional wholesalers, as well as, individual consumers.

The cash and carry approach has evolved over the years, but the defining characteristics remain intact. Operators of cash and carry formats strive to minimise capital costs and operating expenses in order to offer customers the lowest possible cost while achieving an acceptable level of profitability.

Contribution to Retail History

The cash and carry method of retailing represented a major structural change for the wholesale industry and presented a new growth opportunity for the retail industry. As cash and carry steadily gained favour with shoppers it spawned some of the largest and most successful retailers in the process. Today, retailers such as Costco, Sam's Club, Metro and IKEA, operate formats that meet the definition of cash and carry.

Aluminium Can

IN 1959, THE AMERICAN BREWERY, COORS OFFERED CUSTOMERS ONE CENT BACK FOR EACH OF ITS NEW ALL-ALUMINIUM CANS THEY RETURNED. UNLIKE THE TIN AND STEEL CANS THEY REPLACED, THESE WERE TWO-PIECE SEAMLESS DESIGNS WITH THE ADDED BENEFIT OF BEING RECYCLABLE.

Contribution to Retail History

The chilled canned drinks category (comprising both beer and carbonated soft drinks) has become, along with confectionery, coffee and tobacco, one of the underpinnings of the global convenience store industry. Retailers like 7-Eleven and Familymart, not to mention the legions of retail outlets operated by major oil companies, shift billions of beverages in aluminium cans every year. The cans ensure that drinks are kept fresh, hygienic and portable, and are better in terms of logistics, display and multi-pack merchandising than bottles. Recent improvements in design, manufacture and recycling have made canned packaging more efficient than ever.

THESE CANS WERE LIGHTER TOO; THE CAN MANUFACTURERS INSTITUTE ESTIMATES THAT 'FIRST GENERATION' ALUMINIUM CANS WEIGHED THREE OUNCES PER UNIT (TODAY'S CANS WEIGH LESS THAN HALF AN OUNCE).

In 1964, aluminium cans entered the soft drinks market, with RC Cola and Diet Rite being launched by Royal Crown Cola in a two-piece 12oz. aluminium container. These cans were not only a lighter weight, they also had a better surface on which text and graphics could be printed to help reinforce awareness of the brand. In just one year, one million cases of soda were packaged in these new aluminium cans.

In 1967, Coca-Cola and Pepsi-Cola adopted aluminium cans too. But it wasn't until the early 1970s that the aluminium industry launched its 'buy-back' centres, where consumers returned their cans, which were then recycled and returned to the shelves of our stores. This reduced the cost of the original raw materials to the industry and gave us our money back on the cost of our drinks.

The early aluminium cans were opened with a 'church key', a type of can opener. This was followed by the pull-tab, attached at the rivet end, which could be pulled completely off. Its inventor, Ermal Cleon Frazeis, is said to have found himself without his church key during a family picnic, so he used the fender of a car to open his can. In the process he spilled most of the contents. This prompted his creation of the key-free approach. The next adaptation came in 1975 in the form of the 'stay tab' that we recognise today; Daniel Cudzik of Reynolds Metals developed this.

The aluminium can story continues to unfold and its uses to extend. In Nepal in the Himalayas, aluminium cans are the only container allowed because they crush easily and are light. Conversely, in Africa aluminium cans have been used to build what has been described as a 'sturdy hut'.

ATM Machine

WE CALL THEM CASHPOINTS – OR REFER TO THEM AS THE 'HOLE IN THE WALL' BUT THEIR FORMAL NAME IS: 'AUTOMATED TELLER MACHINES'. EARLY PROTOTYPES WEREN'T SUCCESSFUL. IN 1939, LUTHER SIMJIAN, LIVING IN NEW YORK, PATENTED HIS VERSION, THE 'BANKOGRAPH'.

THIS WAS AN AUTOMATED ENVELOPE DEPOSIT MACHINE, WHICH ACCEPTED COINS, CASH AND CHEQUES, BUT IT DID NOT HAVE CASH DISPENSING FEATURES. AN EXPERIMENTAL ONE WAS INSTALLED IN NEW YORK CITY IN 1939, BUT REMOVED AFTER 6 MONTHS, AS CUSTOMERS DID NOT USE IT.

The first ATM was used in 1959 in the Kingsdale Shopping Centre in Upper Arlington, Ohio. Over the next three years many variations on the theme were developed. James Goodfellow of Scotland received a patent in 1966 for his ATM; in 1967, John Shepherd Barron invented and installed an ATM in Barclays Bank in London. A year later, in 1968, Don Wetzel invented an American-made ATM. However, it was not until the late 1980s that ATMs caught on as part of the banking system we have come to know today.

Banks now allow us to insert our 'plastic' with a magnetic strip down the side into the machines and withdraw cash regardless of whether or not we bank with them because the ATMs are connected to inter bank networks. Our pin numbers provide authenticity of who we are.

There 2.2 million ATMs used in the world today, or about one ATM for every 3,000 people. ATMs are not so widely used in the Near East and Africa. India claims to have the world's highest installed ATMs at Nathu La Pass, India, installed by the Union Bank of India at 4,310 metres high. In fact the Agricultural Bank of China has one higher at Nagchu County, Tibet at 4,500 metres high.

Cardless ATMs are next. The RBS and Natwest 'GetCash' mobile apps allow customers who've left their cards behind to request cash and a 6-digit pin will be generated. This code is entered at the ATM, and the funds are dispensed. The transition from a cashless society to a cardless society is underway.

Contribution to Retail History

The ATM liberated shoppers from the tyranny of restrictive banking hours and the necessity of going to a bank to obtain cash. Having the freedom to withdraw funds at any time of day or night extended their ability to shop and spend. The inclusion of ATMs inside stores and shopping centres helps increase spend, as customers are not limited to spending only the cash they have with them. The ATM fuelled the growth of impulse purchasing and being able to take advantage of opportunistic deals from retailers.

Retail Brand

RETAIL BRANDS GO BY DIFFERENT NAMES – PRIVATE LABEL, STORE BRAND OR HOUSE BRAND – BUT THE OBJECTIVE IS SIMILAR. A RETAIL BRAND IS A MEANS BY WHICH TO ACHIEVE COMPETITIVE DIFFERENTIATION, OFFER SHOPPERS AN ENTICING VALUE PROPOSITION, ENHANCE LOYALTY, GENERATE A SUPERIOR RATE OF PROFITABILITY AND GAIN LEVERAGE OVER BRANDED SUPPLIERS.

Retailers employed brand building strategies early in the industry's development as they sought to establish an identity for their stores. The concept of the retailer as a brand gained further traction in the early 20th century when chain stores began expanding more aggressively and needed to cultivate their image with shoppers in new markets. Retail brands came to occupy a special place in the minds of consumers as the businesses they represented tended to be large, successful and regarded as trustworthy.

Beginning in the 1960s, retailers sought to capitalise on that trust through several strategies that helped reshape the industry. Some sought to build entire operations focused on the sale of retail brands or proprietary branded products, examples of which include Germany's Aldi stores and more recently US retailer Supervalu's Sav-A-Lot food stores. The retail brand strategy also became prevalent in the apparel world where companies such as The Gap, H&M and Victoria's Secret achieved success with carefully cultivated brands.

Meanwhile, other retailers infused product assortments long dominated by well-known consumer packaged goods brands with their own retail brands. Early efforts and poor quality generic style products positioned solely as a low cost alternative were unsuccessful, but soon retailers upgraded product quality and began applying the same type of strategies that made national brands successful.

The result was steady market share growth for retail brands in food and in particular, consumable categories. Retail brands are now evident in virtually every merchandise classification and some retailers offer multiple brands within a single category to the detriment of all but the strongest of national and regional brands.

Waitrose

With a 'champagne fizz', sweet **Pink Lady®** apples

LOVE life
1 of your 5 a day
= 1 apple

DISPLAY UNTIL **31 MAY**
SUPPLIER **SUPPLIER 183LSX**
ORIGIN **USA**
CLASS I **68-73mm** x4

EDAM
BUTTE

Sainsbury's
Taste *the*
Difference

Keep ref
Use by

Contribution to Retail History

Retail brands were a game-changing development for the industry. Shoppers' willingness to purchase retail brands and shop at chains dedicated exclusively to particular brands created new avenues of growth and fuelled profitability. Retailers pursued direct manufacturing relationships, acquired established brands outright for their exclusive use and became less reliant on national brands that subjected them to price competition. Retail brands altered the dynamics of retailer and supplier relationships that had existed in the consumer packaged goods world for most of the 20th century, caused huge shifts in market share and contributed to consolidation in the consumer packaged goods world.

BELGIAN DARK
CHOCOLATE &
HAZELNUT COOKIES
ALL BUTTER

TASTE TESTED
BY CUSTOMERS

Sainsbury's
Taste *the*
Difference

TESCO *Finest**

KING SOLOMON
MEDJOOL
DATES

A date contain

Calories	Sugar	Fat	Sa
75	17g	trace	tr
4%	19%	<1%	

of your guideline daily

BEST BEFORE GROWN IN

15 07 2013

Hypermarket

A HYPERMARKET COMBINES THE CONCEPT OF A SUPERMARKET AND A DEPARTMENT STORE INTO ONE. TO BE DEFINED AS A HYPERMARKET THERE MUST BE AT LEAST 150,000 SQUARE FEET OF FLOOR SPACE AND AT LEAST 35% OF THAT SPACE WILL BE USED FOR THE SALE OF NON-FOOD MERCHANDISE.

THERE IS ONE NAME LARGER THAN ALL: WALMART, THE LARGEST HYPERMARKET CHAIN IN THE US, FOLLOWED BY CARREFOUR IN FRANCE. THESE HAVE THE CAPACITY TO STOCK A STAGGERING 200,000 DIFFERENT BRANDS OF GOODS UNDER ONE ROOF.

The concept was first seen in 1934, when Meijer became the first name to open a one-stop shopping centre, selling groceries and drug store goods, with home products and clothing added later. Meijer also had large car parks and a petrol station. It opened its first real 'Supercentre', called 'Thrifty Acres' in Grand Rapids, Michigan, in 1962.

In 1963, Carrefour opened its first Hypermarket at Sainte-Genevieve-des-Bois, France. From 1974 to the 1990s, the Steinberg group had four hypermarkets in Québec. By the late 1980s and early 1990s Walmart, Kmart and Target had set up hypermarkets discounting goods throughout the US. Walmart called their stores Hypermart USA in 1987, and later Walmart Supercenter. Kmart called their stores 'Super Kmart.' In 1995, Dayton-Hudson opened its first SuperTarget store in Omaha, Nebraska. These hypermarkets began to sell fuel too.

Contribution to Retail History

The hypermarket model has grown to dominate the retail landscape globally. The combined food and non-food offering created the efficient one-stop shop and iterations of it have enabled the likes of Carrefour, Auchan, Walmart and Tesco to achieve massive scale. Having been a global phenomenon, the hypermarket in its current form is facing several challenges, not least from the growth of Internet retailing and the time pressure consumers are under.

Intel Chip

WE TAKE FOR GRANTED HOW FAST OUR COMPUTERS AND TECHNOLOGY WORK TODAY. MICROPROCESSORS ('CHIPS') HAVE SPEEDED UP NOT JUST OUR OFFICE AND HOME COMPUTERS BUT THE WORLD OF THE INTERNET TOO.

THEY REPRESENT A HUGE ACHIEVEMENT IN MODERN ENGINEERING AND ONE COMPANY STANDS OUT: INTEL, WHO DEVELOPED THE FIRST MICROPROCESSOR FOR CALCULATORS.

In 1969, Nippon Calculating Machine Corporation asked Intel to design 12 custom chips for its new Busicom 141-PF printing calculator. Intel suggested a family of just four chips, including one that could be used in a variety of products. The four chips were known as the MCS-4: it included a central processing unit chip – the 4004 – as well as supporting a read-only memory chip for the custom applications programmes, a random-access memory chip for processing data and a shift-register chip for the input/output port.

In 1971, Intel purchased the rights to their microprocessor back from Nippon and launched the Intel 4004 processor and its chipset. The advertisement placed in Electronic News on November 15, 1971, announced 'A New Era in Integrated Electronics'. The Intel 4004 processor became the first general-purpose programmable processor on the market. Engineers could use it as a 'building block' to customise their own software, allowing it to perform different functions in a wide variety of electronic devices.

Of its time, the Intel 4004 microprocessor was one of the smallest designs ever commercially produced. To illustrate its power, think about this: the 4004 was the size of a little fingernail, but it could deliver the same computing power as the first electronic computer built in 1946 and that computer occupied an entire room!

Contribution to Retail History

Electronic and computing equipment with the 'Intel Inside®' logo (the famous 'mark' that tells us of the presence of an Intel chip within the device) are used to power the retail supply chain, from end to end. Stock control, distribution, display boards, accounting, online shopping – the entire modern e-commerce process is reliant on microprocessors like these.

EAS Security System

ELECTRONIC ARTICLE SURVEILLANCE (EAS) ARE THE PLASTIC AND METAL SECURITY TAGS THAT ARE FITTED TO GOODS, AND REMOVED OR DEACTIVATED BY THE ASSISTANT AT THE CHECKOUT WHEN THE ITEM IS PURCHASED. IF A TAG IS NOT REMOVED, WHEN THE CUSTOMER TRIES TO LEAVE THE STORE THE SENSORS IN THE DETECTION SYSTEM AT THE EXIT PICK UP THE PRESENCE OF THE TAG AND SOUND AN ALARM TO ALERT STAFF.

EAS systems may be magnetic, acousto-magnetic, radio frequency, microwave, or linked to video surveillance systems. Most clothes retailers now tag their high value products electronically. Such systems save them hundreds of thousands of pounds a year in what would otherwise be lost stock or 'shrinkage' as retailers call this. *Entrepreneur* magazine reported that US businesses lose about $33 billion a year due to theft.

Some manufacturers now fit EAS security tags at source, rather than leaving it to the retailer. Source tagging allows the EAS tags to be concealed and they are more difficult to remove. It also saves the retailer time and costs.

Contribution to Retail History

Retailers of clothing and high value items have always fought a running battle against shoplifters. The EAS system acts as a deterrent to theft of goods, thereby improving retailers' profitability. It also delivers an effective way to catch the perpetrators. Although it still requires security staff to apprehend the potential thief, it enables them to identify them in the act, helping to support subsequent prosecution.

RFID Technology

RADIO FREQUENCY IDENTIFICATION TECHNOLOGY (RFID) USES WIRELESS FREQUENCIES TO TRANSFER ELECTRONICALLY STORED DATA FROM ONE TAGGED ITEM TO SOMEWHERE ELSE. THE TAGS ARE USUALLY EMBEDDED INTO THE TRACKED OBJECT.

TWO-WAY RADIO TRANSMITTER RECEIVERS SEND A SIGNAL TO THE TAG AND READ ITS RESPONSE. RFID TAGS CAN OFTEN ONLY BE READ WITHIN RESTRICTED ZONES. THEY CAN ALSO BE MADE INCREDIBLY SMALL – SCIENTISTS HAVE EVEN GLUED THEM TO ANTS!

Since the Second World War various governments had been experimenting with RFID-like devices for covert listening. But on January 23, 1973, Mario Cardullo patented his 'passive radio transponder' with memory. He had demonstrated it earlier, in 1971, to the New York Port Authority as a device for toll payment.

The RFID system is superior to barcodes, as the tags can be read if they pass near a reader, even if the object is covered or not visible. Tags can also be read when they are inside cases and boxes and the radio transmitter/receiver can read many simultaneously, whereas barcodes can only be read one at a time.

RFID technology is getting cheaper and more reliable to use, leading to a wider use of RFID in industry. Car manufacturers use it to tag a car as it begins the production process and follows it through its various assembly stages to the end. Almost any type of goods can be followed through the supply chain processes using the system. In the fashion industry the RFID label is attached to the garment at the production stage and may be read and traced throughout the entire supply chain, until it is removed at the point-of-sale.

Contribution to Retail History

RFID use in retail is already widespread and multiplying. The tags enable better and more secure stock control for retailers across the supply chain.

Planogram

A TOOL FOR OPTIMISING VISUAL MERCHANDISING IN STORE, THE PLANOGRAM IS A DIAGRAM OR MODEL THAT INDICATES THE PLACEMENT OF RETAIL PRODUCTS ON SHELVES AND THROUGHOUT THE STORE.

A full planogram shows every level of the store. It indicates what is being exhibited on each level, what products are stocked on what shelves and the volume of each product on each shelf. If the rules of the planogram are followed, the theory is that the products' sales and the customer experience are maximised. Kmart is credited with pioneering the planogram.

Sometimes planograms will consist of texts and boxes and others such as those used by clothes manufacturers, may use pictures that show how the products should look when on display. Planograms are often distributed to stores ahead of a new product launch to ensure the product is displayed consistently across each of a store's branches. Retailers use research to decide how best to make use of the available space.

Analysis of past and current sales patterns influence the planogram. For example, the number of 'facings' a certain product should have on display. Margin placement allows the retailer to put those products with a higher profit margin in specific parts of the store and market share placements allow a product to be placed alongside others of a similar nature, decided by how much it's likely to sell.

Planogramming software helps retailers to conduct stocktaking more speedily and accurately and enables virtual teams of manufacturers, retailers, researchers, store managers and of course, the planogrammer, to come together to plan what goes where, in stores all over the globe.

Contribution to Retail History

Made more scientific by the vast quantities of shopping data that is now available, the planogram helps maximise revenues by translating shopper insight gleaned from the data, into the optimum 'on-shelf assortment.'

A diagram or model that indicates the placement of retail products on shelves in order to maximize sales

'Learning From Las Vegas'

'LEARNING FROM LAS VEGAS' BY INFLUENTIAL 20TH CENTURY ARCHITECTS ROBERT VENTURI, DENISE SCOTT BROWN AND STEVEN IZENOUR WAS FIRST PUBLISHED IN 1972 AND IS STILL AVAILABLE IN A REVISED EDITION TODAY.

AN ARCHITECTURAL 'MANIFESTO' AND ENDORSEMENT OF US POPULAR CULTURE, IT USED AN ANALYSIS OF THE BUILDINGS, LIGHTS AND SIGNAGE OF THE LAS VEGAS STRIP TO EXPLORE MODERN DAY ARCHITECTURAL COMMUNICATION.

'Learning from Las Vegas' was produced as a result of a road trip taken by Venturi, Scott Brown, Izenour and a group of their Yale architecture students. On this trip they collected data and photographs and used them to support their argument that the 'decorated shed' (the dominant architectural influence in Las Vegas) was as valid as more orthodox architectural forms.

The book "dismissed the rigid functionalism of International-style modernism in favour of the energetic and spontaneous design eruptions of American car culture, expressed in the neon lights and signs along the Las Vegas Strip."

Although it created a furore when first published, it also helped usher in a new understanding and appreciation of commercial architecture. Venturi Scott Brown and Associates in Philadelphia won numerous awards and honours for their work.

Contribution to Retail History

'Learning from Las Vegas' (LFLV) is a rare thing – an influential polemic from a 'grande' architect in praise of the everyday.

Since the modern built landscape has come to be greatly influenced by the architecture, design and communications of the shopping experience, the LFLV 'manifesto' gave a welcome recognition to the role of 'retail vernacular' in helping to shape social culture.

Loyalty Card

THE LOYALTY CARD IS AN ICONIC SYMBOL OF A MARKETING STRATEGY WHICH IS WIDESPREAD WITHIN THE RETAIL INDUSTRY.

SHOPPERS EMBRACED RETAILERS' LOYALTY CARDS AS A MEANS TO OBTAIN A WIDE RANGE OF REWARDS BASED ON THEIR LEVEL EXPENDITURES WHILE RETAILERS COVETED THE WEALTH OF SHOPPER INSIGHTS DATA GENERATED BY CARD USAGE TO HELP DEVELOP MORE EFFECTIVE PROMOTIONAL STRATEGIES.

American Airlines is credited with the development of the first loyalty programme in 1981, but retailers were not far behind in recognising the business value associated with rewarding their best customers. This was especially true of retailers operating in a consumer packaged goods marketplace, characterised by an abundance of retail outlets and intense price competition. These factors made attracting and retaining shoppers key business considerations. The loyalty card represented a way for retailers to enhance their value proposition and establish differentiation with shoppers.

Today it seems at times that virtually every retailer offers some form of a branded loyalty programme with incentive structures that vary widely to include cashback offers, reduced prices, percentage discounts, access to special promotions, free shipping of online orders or the ability to accrue points that can be redeemed for merchandise.

Although retailers and their trading partners incur costs associated with loyalty cards, the expense is justified by the wealth of purchase behaviour data generated by card usage. The data allows retailers to know the intimate details of shoppers' purchase behaviour and in turn more precisely target shoppers or shopper segments with relevant offers to drive even greater loyalty. Increasingly powerful data analytics capabilities now give retailers the ability to blend loyalty card usage information with other data streams to develop an even deeper understanding of shopper behaviour.

Today, loyalty cards are so prevalent that retailers are challenged to develop ever richer reward structures to drive participation and usage among shoppers whose pocketbooks are stuffed with loyalty cards.

Contribution to Retail History

The loyalty card changed retailers' approach to marketing and introduced a new competitive dynamic to the industry. Retailers sought to devise and promote branded loyalty offerings with incentive structures optimised to drive participation and shopping frequency. In the process, a new type of value proposition was created that required shoppers to assess the value of loyalty card benefits in determining where to shop.

'I Shop Therefore I Am'

AMERICAN CONCEPTUAL ARTIST, BARBARA KRUGER, BEGAN HER CAREER WORKING FOR MAGAZINES IN THE LATE 1960s AND THIS EXPOSURE TO FASHION AND THE REVOLUTIONARY CULTURE OF THE ERA STRONGLY INFLUENCED HER WORK.

SHE WAS MUCH ACCLAIMED FOR HER ARRANGEMENTS OF IMAGE WITH TEXT AND COMPLETED MANY ADVERTISING COMMISSIONS.

Kruger became most famous for her work that showed pictures (often in black and white) with slogans or words that highlighted the failings in society at the time. Her pop art frequently dealt with consumerism and feminism. She began by coining phrases such as "Your comfort is my silence" in 1981, and in 1982, "You invest in the divinity of the masterpiece."

In 1987, she produced a screen print with the words "I shop, therefore I am." It was a statement on power and sexism in modern society. That one phrase defined us as shoppers and the explosion of retail in a secular age that lived by the values of shopping too. Kruger explained her work by saying: "I work with pictures and words because they have the ability to determine who we are and who we aren't."

Her profound 'definition' of the human race as shoppers was a deliberate play on the words of the French philosopher René Descartes who famously said: "Cogito ergo sum" ("I think therefore I am"). Today, other people also adopt and adapt these words, with slogans such as "I blog therefore I am" or "I drink therefore I am."

Kruger has forever defined who we are in relation to our huge thirst for shopping and 'our favoured brands' which identify who we are.

Contribution to Retail History

Few are likely to concur that the act of shopping defines their existence, but most would agree that we are defined by the brands we buy. In the 1960s the power of the brand was rising and retail increasingly became about selling a lifestyle, as well as a product.

In-Store Television

RETAILERS USE IN-STORE TELEVISION TO INFLUENCE SHOPPERS AT THE POINT OF PURCHASE. SCREENS OF VARYING SIZES STRATEGICALLY LOCATED IN KEY AREAS ALLOW FOR TARGETED MESSAGING TO DRIVE PURCHASE INTENT OF FEATURED ITEMS AND CATEGORIES.

IN-STORE TELEVISION SYSTEMS ALSO ALLOW RETAILERS TO SHOW CONTENT OF INTEREST TO THE LOCAL COMMUNITY TO ENCOURAGE LOYALTY.

Technological advancements such as the barcode and point-of-sale scanning provided retailers with a wealth of data regarding sales and product performance. These new sources of data were robust and insightful when it came to understanding historical sales trends, but did little to advance knowledge regarding how to influence shoppers on their path to purchase. Extensive study of consumer behaviour prior to arriving at the store led to the view that many purchase decisions were made in store while shoppers stood at the shelf.

Consequently, retailers and brands directed considerable energy against influencing customers while they shopped. It was this desire that led to the development of in-store television. Early versions introduced in the 1990s seemed innovative at the time, but rapid advancements in technology meant large analog boxes used to display content had to be upgraded to higher resolution flat panel screens. Retailers experimented with screen sizes and locations throughout the store with some opting to integrate screens into endcaps where messaging could be surrounded by the featured product.

The use of this type of in-store television was limited to all but the largest retailers who had sufficient means to make the sizable investment to install, maintain, operate, periodically upgrade the technology and cope with the increased operational complexity.

Contribution to Retail History

In-store television gave retailers and brands a new way to communicate with shoppers at the point-of-purchase. The availability of in-store television networks at some of the world's largest retailers caused brands to reallocate ad budgets and devise new marketing strategies to communicate with shoppers at store entrances, in aisles and at the checkout.

www.retail100objects.com

Internet

THE ORIGINS OF THE INTERNET DATE BACK TO THE 1960s WHEN THE US GOVERNMENT BEGAN RESEARCH INTO COMPUTER NETWORKS. THE SUBSEQUENT DEVELOPMENT OF INTERCONNECTED NETWORKS FIRST ALLOWED RESEARCHERS TO SHARE INFORMATION, BUT BY THE 1990s THE COMMERCIAL POTENTIAL OF THE TECHNOLOGY HAD BECOME EVIDENT.

The Internet gained mass market appeal in the mid-1990s and usage of it has grown exponentially ever since. More than one-third of the global population now accesses the Internet and the figure continues to rise, creating new operational challenges and unprecedented growth opportunities for retailers.

The Internet offers shoppers unprecedented access to information, the ability to consume, share and create content and engage in commerce like never before. Presented with this collection of amazing capabilities, the Internet quickly gained popularity. The introduction of devices which allow for mobile access made the Internet an indispensable part of daily life and transformed the retail industry in the process.

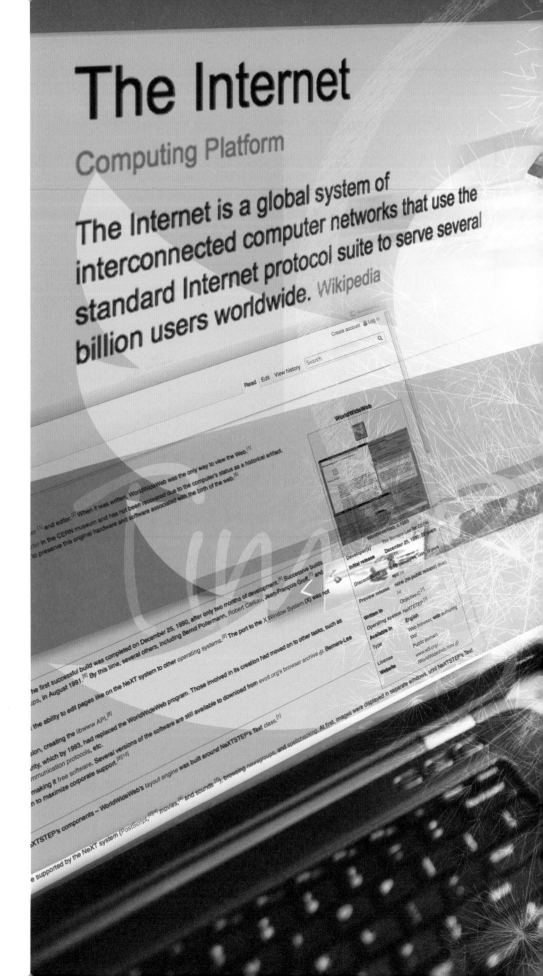

amazon.com

It is a phenomenon best exemplified by Amazon.com. Founded in 1995, Amazon.com's initial focus on books and music soon expanded to include other categories and new geographies. The company was the first to recognise and harness the power of user-generated content in the form of product reviews. Shoppers loved reading others' reviews and contributing their own. This unique attribute and Amazon.com's site functionality, commitment to supply chain logistics and customer service, were a potent combination.

As assortments were expanded and more product reviews followed, Amazon began to rival Google as a place where shoppers began their search for products. Traffic to the company's website now routinely exceeds 100 million unique monthly visitors. Annual sales last year increased 27% to slightly more than $61 billion and more growth is expected as the company executes a vision of being the world's most customer-centric company and a place where shoppers can buy virtually anything at the lowest possible price.

Internet

WHILE AMAZON.COM WAS BUSY LEVERAGING THE INTERNET TO HELP SHOPPERS BUY, EBAY WAS FOCUSED ON THE SELL SIDE OF THE COMMERCE EQUATION.

The company launched its online auction platform in 1995 and quickly gained favour with sellers and buyers. The auction approach evolved into something much more significant and soon encompassed all aspects of commerce. Many users sold directly, foregoing the auction process entirely, to establish digital storefronts, in essence making eBay the equivalent of the world's largest online mall. The company enables users to buy and sell in nearly every country and through its PayPal subsidiary it facilitates the ability to securely send and receive payments.

Today, eBay is the second most heavily trafficked e-commerce site on the Internet and generates annual revenues of slightly more than $14 billion.

The likes of eBay, Amazon and other online-only retailers were at one point regarded as a death knell for traditional brick and mortar chains, especially those who offered categories that were well-suited to online purchasing. However, retailers such as Walmart, Tesco, Costco and Macy's recognised their physical stores were not the liability some believed them to be during the Internet's heady early years. Faced with a new breed of competitor and shopper expectations that were being elevated

higher and faster than ever before, conventional retailers adopted a blended approach to serving shoppers that came to be known as 'multichannel retailing'.

In Walmart's case, it recognised its physical store base which exceeds 4,000 units in the US alone could be used as miniature fulfilment centres. The company acquired e-commerce capabilities domestically and internationally and created a global e-commerce group charged with transforming the Internet into a new growth engine for the company. As things stand now, Walmart.com is the third most frequently visited retail site on the Internet and routinely averages more than 40 million unique visitors each month. Its online sales total roughly $10 billion, a fraction of total revenues of nearly $470 billion.

However, as Walmart and other conventional retailers have discovered, one of the realities of an increasingly multichannel world is that attributing a sale to a store, a website or a mobile device is irrelevant. Shoppers don't care how a retailer accounts for the sale – only that all platforms and points of interaction with the retailer are highly integrated so as to provide a seamless experience with the brand.

www.retail100objects.com

Contribution to Retail History

The Internet's contribution to retail history is impossible to overstate and far from complete. In roughly 15 years, the Internet spawned disruptive companies such as Amazon, eBay, Google, Facebook, Twitter and Alibaba. The growth the Internet allowed these companies to achieve changed everything retailers thought they knew about retail. From the sourcing and development of merchandise, to marketing communications, store operations and supply chain logistics, retailers were forced to cope with an unprecedented pace of change.

Retailers' boardroom conversations were dominated by discussions of e-commerce, multichannel integration and how to serve customers' rapidly advancing expectations. Traditional retailers were forced to adjust to new marketplace dynamics created by online only retailers who were gaining market share at an alarming pace, while conventional retailers were shifting to an integrated model that leveraged physical assets and the trust of well-established brand identities.

The Internet's contribution to retail history remains a work in progress as innovative companies seem to reinvent the future daily. However, an enduring contribution promises to be one of consumer empowerment and access to limitless possibilities. That is the new expectation of shoppers in the digital age and the competitive climate in which retailers now operate thanks to behaviours, communications and lifestyle choices that didn't exist a generation ago. For many people, anytime, anywhere access to the Internet and the ability to purchase a limitless assortment of products is now taken for granted in much the same way as electricity, indoor plumbing and air travel.

Chip & PIN

WE STAND AT THE CHECKOUT OR AT AN ATM, INSERT OUR CARDS INTO A SLOT AND KEY IN OUR FOUR DIGIT CHIP & PIN NUMBERS TO WITHDRAW FUNDS OR PAY FOR GOODS OR SERVICES.

THE CHIP IS EMBEDDED INTO OUR CARD AND THE PIN IS OUR PERSONAL IDENTIFICATION NUMBER AND BOTH HAVE TO BE USED IN COMBINATION. THE CHIP HOLDS THE SAME PERSONAL DATA AS THE MAGNETIC STRIPE – CUSTOMER NAME, CARD NUMBER, EXPIRY DATE – BUT IT IS SECURED USING ADVANCED ENCRYPTION.

During the course of the early 1990s and early 21st century, most of Western Europe, Australia, and New Zealand began to adopt Chip & PIN smartcards (the US has yet to adopt it, although Canada has begun the migration). The system replaced the old cards with magnetic stripes down the sides, which had to be validated with a customer signature. These gave rise to security concerns including forged signatures and the ability for employees to swipe transactions through fraudulently when they took customers' cards out of sight. Chip & PIN technology quickly became an established standard for safety and security for card transactions, providing enhanced protection against fraud from lost, stolen, and counterfeit cards. When France introduced the system around 1993 it saw card fraud drop by 80%.

With the introduction of Chip & PIN, responsibility for paying the cost of fraudulent transactions passed from the issuing bank to the retailers themselves, thus giving retailers an incentive to upgrade to the new technology. These days, banks have to prove that the cardholder is at fault if fraud does take place, rather than assuming that it is the customer's fault.

The advent of Chip & PIN technology coincided with the advances in wireless data communication, enabling the card reader system to be portable. For example, in restaurants, the card need never leave the customer's sight.

Contribution to Retail History

A key development in the move to a cashless society, Chip & PIN made customer transactions and back office accounting and reconciliation much easier for retailers. In reducing fraud (theft of cash or from staff 'skimming' information from customers' cards) the system has also lowered retailers' costs. The ease of use of Chip & PIN and the fact that there is no 'minimum' spend per transaction has encouraged customers to use them for even small impulse purchases that they might otherwise not have made.

QR STANDS FOR QUICK RESPONSE, AND IT IS THE NAME GIVEN TO A TWO-DIMENSIONAL BARCODE STYLE RECOGNITION SYSTEM.

QR Code

QR CODES USE SQUARE BLACK DOTS ARRANGED ON A GRID ON A WHITE BACKGROUND, AND HAVE A GREATER CAPACITY FOR STORING INFORMATION THAN THE TRADITIONAL BARCODE. ORIGINALLY DESIGNED FOR USE WITHIN THE JAPANESE AUTOMOTIVE INDUSTRY, OVER THE PAST FEW YEARS THE USE OF QR CODES HAS BECOME MORE WIDESPREAD.

Today, retailers and consumers can 'read' QR codes using a handheld device such as a smartphone. The camera on the device takes an image of the code and underlying software extracts the data that is represented in the 'patterns' of the code, to return information to the user. The codes can also be used to launch videos, send a text, or direct the viewer to a website. Applications of the QR to date include product tracking, document management and marketing communications.

QR codes have the potential to take online shopping to new heights, as illustrated by Tesco's recent development in South Korea. The grocery retailer produced a 'virtual store' on a wall, displaying products with QR codes under each. Customers simply 'read' the QR code with their smartphone to add selected purchases to their online shopping basket, for subsequent home delivery.

Contribution to Retail History

It's still relatively early days for QR codes and they are taking a long time to gain traction. However, as smartphone penetration continues to increase it is likely that the codes – or ones based on similar principles – will have an important part to play in the evolution of consumers' searching and shopping habits, allowing more information to be communicated to help inform decision making and in assisting in more online purchases.

Smartphone

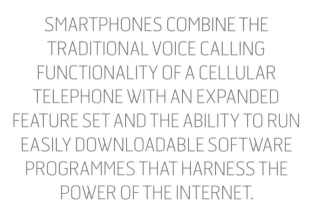

SMARTPHONES ARE POWERFUL TOOLS FOR SHOPPING THAT GIVE USERS UNPRECEDENTED ACCESS TO INFORMATION AND THE ABILITY TO INSTANTLY COMMUNICATE WITH A GLOBAL AUDIENCE VIA SOCIAL MEDIA.

The earliest devices to combine telephony and computing emerged in the early to mid-1990s and were produced by IBM and Nokia. However, the phrase "smartphone" didn't appear until 1997 when Ericsson introduced a concept product billed as a smart phone. A few years later it began actively marketing several products as smartphones and then in 2002 the Blackberry arrived on the scene and quickly gained acceptance among business users who found its email functionality addictive.

While these early models possessed various smart phone attributes, it wasn't until 2007 with the introduction of Apple's iPhone that the smartphone revolution began. The iPhone's ease of use, feature set, elegant design, touch screen user interface and most importantly, abundance of applications, made the product an instant hit. Apple fans clamoured for upgrades of the original model and soon other handset manufacturers introduced competing products with similar feature sets running on alternative operating systems. Smartphone sales quickly outpaced those of conventional handsets and in the span of less than six years the smartphone penetration rate had surpassed 50% and was climbing steadily.

SMARTPHONES COMBINE THE TRADITIONAL VOICE CALLING FUNCTIONALITY OF A CELLULAR TELEPHONE WITH AN EXPANDED FEATURE SET AND THE ABILITY TO RUN EASILY DOWNLOADABLE SOFTWARE PROGRAMMES THAT HARNESS THE POWER OF THE INTERNET.

As smartphones became an integral part of daily life for millions of people, the capabilities the devices offered shoppers created new challenges and opportunities for retailers. Retailers offered apps that allowed shoppers to connect with their brand, locate stores, purchase products, create shopping lists, track online orders and receive marketing communications such as incentives or product recommendations. Smartphones also gave shoppers the ability to instantly compare prices while standing in store aisles and provided access to product reviews which could impact sales.

Smartphones have had a tremendous impact on the retail industry in a compressed period of time, but even greater change is expected as new shoppers join the mobile revolution. The capabilities of smartphones are advancing, download speeds and wireless access are improving and form factors are evolving to include the emerging genre of wearable devices. The impact of smartphones and all manner of internet-enabled mobile devices on the retail industry is just beginning.

Contribution to Retail History

The smartphone gave shoppers an unprecedented ability to access and share information via a mobile device with significant implications for retailers. Most notably, smartphones brought an unprecedented level of price transparency to the shopper and spawned the practice of "showrooming," where in-store prices are instantly compared to online competitors. Retailers capitalised on the power of smartphones by introducing their own apps with extensive functionality to enhance shopping and some retailers even equipped employees with smartphones that ran company-specific apps to aid in customer service operations. The smartphone forced retailers to move faster than at any time in history to keep pace with the elevating expectations of a new generation of shoppers accustomed to life with a smartphone.

6
Future Objects

A glimpse of the retail future through objects not yet invented or commercialised

BRIAN DAVID JOHNSON
Futurist, The Intel Corporation

and

DAVID ROTH
CEO, The Store WPP, EMEA and Asia

SCAN WITH
layar

What do you think the future will be like? When you imagine tomorrow what do you see? Do you see jet packs and flying cars? Is your future a utopia of possibilities or a dark dystopia of events gone horribly wrong? Are you ready for the future?

Well, the future isn't what it used to be.

We find ourselves in an amazing time. Our science and technology have progressed to the point where what we build is only limited by our own imaginations. No longer do we need to sit back and passively accept the future. We can build it.

This is why imagining and exploring the future is so important. To envision the future of retail we used a process called 'futurecasting'. It's a mix of social science, technical research, economics, statistical data, global interviews and even a little science fiction to model what it will feel like to live and shop 10 to 20 years from now. The goal of the process is to create a realistic, fact- based vision for the future that we can then go and build.

As we set about 'futurecasting' the future of retail, we quickly saw that the experience of shopping really hasn't changed that much. Stretching back in history, the human experience of shopping has remained remarkably the same. What has changed over the years are the objects that fill that experience. This is why we found the 'History of Retail in 100 Objects' project so fascinating and revealing. The history and the future of retail can be told best through the objects that have and will enrich the shopping experience.

To best explain the future of retail, we developed and created new models and frameworks to illuminate each part of the sometimes complex and varied shopping experience for the future. We broke the experience of retail into three sections: the face, the bones and the brain. These three parts make up a person's holistic experience.

THE FACE OF RETAIL

Whether it's browsing in a store or clicking through a website, the Face of Retail captures what we will all see when we shop. How will the physical and visual experience of shopping grow and evolve with the introduction of new technologies and gadgets?

THE BONES OF RETAIL

Underneath the visible world lies a vast and complex network that enables the world of retail. These infrastructures and supply chains, fuelled by innovation and striving for efficiency, are the engines of the industry.

THE BRAINS OF RETAIL

Retail has always had 'big data' but with increasing computational intelligence the industry will become smarter and more responsive than ever. The Brains of Retail will open up new opportunities, enriching the experience of shoppers and deepening the connection to employees.

The future is not an accident. The future doesn't just happen. The future is not what it used to be. The future is built every day by the actions of people and businesses. 'Future Objects' give us a glimpse into that future. Let's imagine what it will feel like to be a consumer and shop in the future. Let's ask ourselves what kind of future we want. Can we challenge ourselves to imagine a radically different future to what we have today? Can we see a more prosperous, sustainable and mindful tomorrow?

You will build and shape the future of retail but you have to imagine it first.

The Face of Retail

Holostores

THE VIABILITY OF HOLOGRAPHIC TECHNOLOGY IS DRAWING EVER CLOSER DUE TO TECHNOLOGICAL ADVANCEMENTS IN 3D CAMERAS, SUFFICIENT COMPUTATIONAL PERFORMANCE, ADVANCED COMPRESSION ALGORITHMS, IMPROVED BROADBAND SPEED, AND HOLOGRAPHIC DISPLAY.

Holograms will be used in-store to deepen the customer experience. Aside from being a high-end draw for shoppers, retailers will be able to integrate them as part of the physical store to create virtual environments. Shelving may not be physical but a fully digital display of current products and offers. Retailers will no longer be bound by capital expenditure to update stores, as daily updates and rearrangement of the store will now be possible. The photon will replace the euro hook.

Whether a few centimetres high and projected on the counter top, or several metres in height and used in windows or in-store display, 3D projections will play through scenarios, ask the customer questions, and respond accordingly. Using Big Data and information held on the individual's smart device, the holograms will be programmed to interact and deliver calls to action based on the customer's history and preferences.

Use of holograms in the home will also prompt greater consumer engagement and such a volumetric display would remove many of the physical retailing setbacks for home commerce. Consumers would be able to see, accurately assess dimensions and possibly touch (using developments in haptic sensory feedback), any product that they are viewing online.

Intelligent Shelves

HOW MANY TIMES HAVE YOU LOOKED
FOR A PRODUCT IN A STORE, ONLY TO BE
CONFUSED BY THE MANY SIZES, OPTIONS AND
ATTRIBUTES OF ALL THE OPTIONS AVAILABLE?

Statistics show that on average, consumers are hesitant to try new products, making it a challenge for manufacturers to introduce new offerings successfully. To turn this around, brands and retailers are looking at 'Intelligent Shelving' solutions to provide eye-catching digital graphic displays right next to new products, which increase awareness and encourage consumers to try them. The solutions can inform shoppers about special promotions (70% of purchase decisions are made at the point-of-sale itself), and in doing so, move products that are nearing their sell-by date, thus reducing the amount of product lost to waste.

Anonymous Viewer Analytics technology can be used to gather anonymous consumer data, such as age and gender, at the point-of-sale which can then be used to analyse buying patterns and optimise promotion strategies and inventory. Imagine these scenarios...if you own a 2007 Honda Accord and need an air filter, intelligent shelves can detect your presence and highlight the proper product's price tag. If you have nut allergies, the shelves will highlight the products containing nuts. If you've recently purchased salmon, the shelves will highlight the wines that make a good accompaniment...

These intelligent shelves can serve as a link between 'experience shopping' and the purchase of Soft Goods or even Fast Moving Consumer Goods such as food or beverage. Ideally, the intelligent shelves could transform 'get it done' activities to a more social and meaningful shopping experiences.

Intelligent shelves will also link to the infrastructure of the store; in-built sensors will enable the shelves to understand their stock level and know when to send an automated request for replenishment.

The Face of Retail

Smart Clothing/Intelligent Fashion

Bio Sensors will be built into clothing in response to the growing desire to be able to 'quantify self'. Sensors in garments will track the wearer's physical and mental state, for example, monitoring blood pressure, heart rate, temperature, blood sugar level, sleep patterns.

Similarly, social sensors will be embedded in clothing and will alert you to opportunities and developments in your immediate vicinity, communicating with social networks to tell you, for example, when your friends are nearby. Retail networks will be able to communicate with customers in the same way; gathering data on their preferences, shareable information and secure purchasing information.

Personal Flexible Augmented Viewer

As the concept of a standalone personal computing device diminishes, computing will be everywhere and information accessible from almost any environment. Yet the need for a portable, personal screen to view content will be as important as ever. Flexible and foldable displays will allow a tiny item to transform into a large screen. These convenient screens will fold or roll up or be worn comfortably to be deployed easily by the user when any form of personal visual interaction is required.

In-store, full-size screens will be lightweight and adaptable enough to use as promotional flags and banners. Such displays will be quick and easy to update and move around the store, creating a more immersive experiential environment.

The viewer is no bigger than a pen but can be pulled open and its bistable mechanism rigidifies the screen to create a large display.

The Bones of Retail

Drones

Drones will have a part to play in several key stages of the supply chain. As intelligent autonomous machines, they will allow retailers to operate with greater computational intelligence in the real world, getting to places and spaces that would be impossible for human employees. From monitoring the environment and stock levels within all areas of a warehouse, to implementing the 'last mile' personal delivery service to customers, drones will be both reconnaissance and 'dropship' carrier vehicles.

Personal 3D Printing

Before the modern age, many of us were defined by what we made. Do you know anyone named Smith? Or Mason? Or Cobbler? Products were made by someone in the community with the creativity to design and the knowledge to build. Creativity and production resided together in the forges and shops of a creative artisan class. Goods were produced specifically to the needs of the customer.

Mass manufacturing prompted a redefinition. Specialisation meant that creativity and production split into separate groups. Both became cogs in the factories. Products were produced for the masses instead of for the individual. Massive distribution systems were built to deliver the benefits of economies of scale and mass manufacturing.

3D Printing and advances in other fabrication and distribution technologies will create another shift in the relationship between creators, producers and consumers. Markets are now emerging where creators and designers sell their designs without ever producing or manufacturing anything.

Production can exist anywhere, so design can be localised to the needs of the community. Products can be designed and then redesigned by the individual.

Distribution systems designed for concentrated centralised production, will be optimised for faster delivery of products produced around the corner, instead of around the world. As more products become uniquely produced for the individual, the need for retailers to carry inventory will diminish but the opportunity for them to offer 'print on demand' will grow.

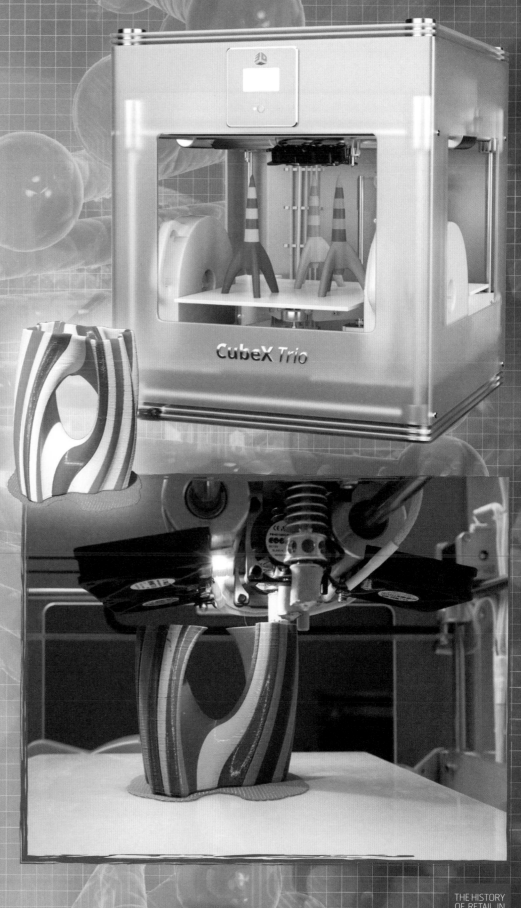

The Bones of Retail

Flooring adapts to guide customers

Personalised signage

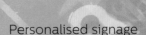

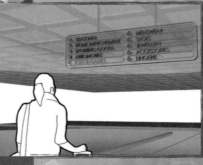

Directed individual sound for information or entertainment

Sentient Stores

The store of the future will not only have a brain but will also sense. Able to adapt to individual consumers or manage groups, the integration of intelligence through computing and sensory feedback will enable a deeper level of retail experience.

Stores will be able to manage the flow of customers through the environment and individually target a customer with offers. The consumer will experience accurate guidance and product information. The store will be able to promote products according to the individual's preferences and where those products are located in relation to the shopper's current position. Stock levels, down to the smallest detail, will be monitored and replenished automatically. Shopping will be frustration-free, retailers will be much more efficient, and marketing more targeted and effective.

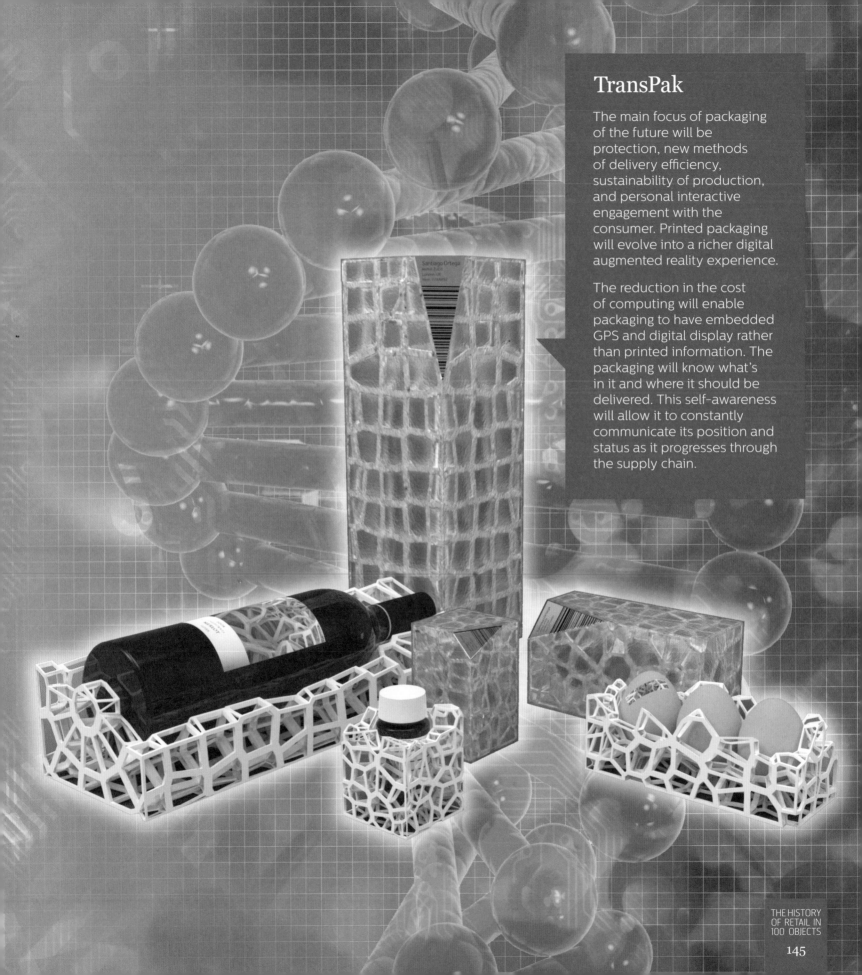

TransPak

The main focus of packaging of the future will be protection, new methods of delivery efficiency, sustainability of production, and personal interactive engagement with the consumer. Printed packaging will evolve into a richer digital augmented reality experience.

The reduction in the cost of computing will enable packaging to have embedded GPS and digital display rather than printed information. The packaging will know what's in it and where it should be delivered. This self-awareness will allow it to constantly communicate its position and status as it progresses through the supply chain.

The Brains of Retail

The Secret Life of Data

IN THE AGE OF BIG DATA AND THE MATURATION OF ITS USAGE, RETAILERS WILL DEPLOY ALGORITHMS TO PROCESS AND UNDERSTAND THE BUSINESS INTELLIGENCE THE DATA CAPTURES.

Optimisation will be used to handle data relating to every stage of the supply chain – from choice of designs, production quantities, storage, marketing, display and delivery.

Data and how to use it effectively and responsibly will radically change the landscape of retail. One area of significant impact will be how digital consumers enrich their shopping experiences and improve their daily lives and communities with data.

Shopping is often a social activity. With the rise in popularity of Internet-based social networks, we cannot only shop with our friends but our data can shop with our friends' data. The store's data can interact with the social fabric of the customers to create more informed, personalised shopping experiences, as well as, offering socially appropriate options. Further, by combining personal

or local data with the vast and varied sources of data, a new value can be created.

Companies like Nike are developing new personal data tracking devices and working to provide users with data collection services to let them learn more and more about themselves and each other. For example, users might map their own personal run data against that of others, using a run tracking device like Nike+. Or they might map their personal run data against city data on hiking trails or air quality data from the Environmental Protection Agency to understand the safest days for a run in an urban location.

A user's data can connect with other people they know and create bundles tailored to them. For example, they were going to buy a lawn trimmer but if they add a power washer like their neighbours have, they'll

get a discount. Or, conversely, 'don't buy the same dress that your friend just did – here are some alternative options'. Data can also connect consumers to people they don't know but who have similar tastes. Data can lead to a personalised shopping experience such coupons, discounts and other targeted incentives. User's data can also be combined with others to get a buying pool. A retailer sees there is a group of new parents in a user's area, so invites them in with discounted prams, or a group of new home owners are offered a discount on home appliances.

In summary, data will interact across all stages of the consumer purchase journey. Every individual will have a data avatar that embodies their social and purchasing persona; retailers will engage with this data to optimise selling and marketing opportunities, irrespective of time or place.

BRANDZ™ Insight

The omni-channel world challenges retailers

Amazon became the BrandZ Most Valuable Global Retail Brand in 2013, ahead of Walmart, showing that the history of retail is constantly evolving and the importance of digital growing.

The resurgent US economy drove an impressive 17 percent brand value growth in the retail category in 2013. Brand value declined 5 percent a year ago. But the US was only part of the story. Brand became a more important tool for differentiating retail organisations and attracting consumers who shopped anytime, anywhere, often on mobile devices, even visiting more than one location simultaneously. Retailers developed brand ecosystems for reaching consumers in a unified way across all channels. To draw traffic and build loyalty, retailers worked to improve the in-store brand experience. The impact of all of these initiatives varied across geographic regions and store formats. Brands with a major presence in Europe, especially hypermarkets and food retailers, felt the impact of the Continent's financial troubles.

The Top 20 Most Valuable Global Retail Brands comes from the BrandZ Top 100 Most Valuable Global Brands 2013. To download a full copy of the BrandZ Top 100 Most Valuable Global Brands 2013 go to www.Brandz.com

The Top 20 Most Valuable Global Retail Brands

		Brand value 2013 $M	Brand contribution	Brand value % change 2013 vs 2012
1	Amazon	45,727	3	34%
2	Walmart	36,220	2	5%
3	The Home Depot	18,488	2	43%
4	eBay	17,749	2	40%
5	Tesco	16,303	4	-9%
6	IKEA	12,040	3	31%
7	Target	11,879	3	13%
8	Woolworths	11,039	3	New
9	Aldi	8,885	2	-5%
10	Lowe's	7,559	2	26%
11	Carrefour	7,372	2	-6%
12	Costco	6,789	2	33%
13	Whole Foods	6,728	4	New
14	Walgreens	5,925	2	New
15	CVS	5,620	3	New
16	Falabella	5,611	5	7%
17	M&S	4,649	3	7%
18	Asda	4,617	3	19%
19	Lidl	4,524	2	-2%
20	Coles	4,416	3	New

Valuations include data from BrandZ™, Kantar Worldpanel, Kantar Retail and Bloomberg.
Brand Contribution measures the influence of brand alone on earnings, on a scale of 1 to 5 (5 highest).

Ancient retail objects transformed by brands in the modern era

The time of invention for retail objects goes back to pre-historic times, but the application for consumers is brought to life in strong brands, particularly in the modern era.

The oldest brand in the BrandZ Top 100 Most Valuable Brands ranking is Chase Bank (started in 1799) most surely a sophisticated version of the Neolithic invented abacus. The most modern brand is Facebook (2004).

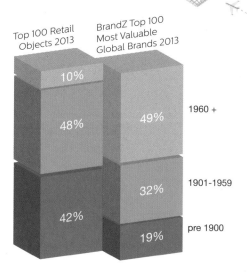

Top 100 Retail Objects 2013 — 10%, 48%, 42%

BrandZ Top 100 Most Valuable Global Brands 2013 — 49% (1960 +), 32% (1901-1959), 19% (pre 1900)

BRANDZ™ - Helping develop strong brands

Like any great brand, BrandZ™ stands apart from its competition because it's relevant and meaningful to its customers. Constantly updated, the propitiatory BrandZ™ big data includes in-depth quantitative research with more than two million consumers.

We examine 10,000+ brands in over 30 countries every year. This rigorous approach is unique to BrandZ™. The BrandZ™ analytic database has yielded insights into the causal links between brand strength, sales and profits. We use this powerful proprietary WPP resource to help our clients build and sustain great local and global brands.

The definitive BRANDZ™ brand valuation methodology

Brand owners and members of the financial community rely on BrandZ™ for the most objective and reliable brand valuations. Like all valuation methodologies, BrandZ™ begins with sophisticated financial analysis. We first determine how much of corporate earnings can be specifically attributed to the brand. But then we go further, much further than any other methodologies, to understand the power of brand where it most counts — in the mind of the consumer. For this critical step we rely on the world's largest brand analytic database, BrandZ™, to objectively measure the Brand Contribution.

To learn more about BrandZ™ brand valuations email Elspeth Cheung at Elspeth.cheung@millwardbrown.com

To download a full copy of the BrandZ™ Top 100 Most Valuable Global Brands 2013 go to www.Brandz.com

Acknowledgements

Advisory Board

PROFESSOR RODNEY FITCH CBE
Retail and Design Consultant and Professor
of Retail Innovation and Complimentary Studies
at TU Delft University

ANDREW A. GRANT
Chairman, Satalia Optimisation

SIR THOMAS BLANE HUNTER
Founder and Chairman
West Coast Capital

PROFESSOR JEREMY MYERSON
Director, The Helen Hamlyn Centre for Design,
Royal College of Art

PROFESSOR PETER NOLAN CBE
Chong Hua Professor and
Director, Centre of Development Studies,
University of Cambridge

BRYAN ROBERTS
Retail Insights Director, Kantar Retail

DAVID ROTH
CEO, The Store WPP, EMEA and Asia

DAVID L. SISSON
Head of Global Real Estate/Properties,
Best Buy Co., Inc

MATTHEW EDWARD THOMAS WHITE
Design and Engineering Director,
SPARK Product Creation Ltd

WILLIAM JOHN WHITING
Retired, formerly Chief Executive of B&Q plc
and Executive Director of Kingfisher plc

From Intel Corporation:

JOE JENSEN
General Manager, Retail Solutions Division

JOSE AVALOS
Worldwide Director, Visual Retail

BRIAN DAVID JOHNSON
Futurist & Principal Engineer

MAROUN ISHAC
Business Development

INTEL CORPORATION PROJECT SUPPORT TEAM

STEVE BROWN – Chief Evangelist and Futurist
ADRIAN WHELAN – Embedded Business Development Director
DANIEL BROOKES – Embedded Retail Operations
MEGAN BEDNARZ – End User/Ecosystem/Channel Enablement
ANDREA QUOCK – Program Manager
ELAINE COOK – EMEA Retail Marketing Manager
DAVID HARRISON – Program Manager

CONTRIBUTORS

HELEN BARRACLOUGH
Senior Legal Counsel , WPP

CAROLYN CUMMINGS-OSMOND
MA Coordinator & Senior Lecturer
Southampton Solent University

TAMSIN GRANT
Wordscout

DANIELA HORNSKOV SUN
The Store WPP

NICOLA MCCORMICK
Michael Simkins LLP

BONI SONES OBE
Executive Producer at
www.bonisonesproductions.com

JAMES SORENSEN
Senior Vice President
Retail and Shopper, TNS

MIKE TROY
Editor-in-Chief, Retailing Today

PETER WALSHE
Global BrandZ Director, Millward Brown

PROJECT MANAGEMENT

AMANDA HARRISON
The Store WPP

DESIGN AND PRODUCTION

KAY BLEWETT
Bauernhaus Creative

PHOTOGRAPHY

CECILIE ØSTERGREN
www.ostergren.dk

Cecilie Østergren is a professional photographer, based in Shanghai, who has worked closely with WPP agencies since 2009. Cecilie specialises in documentary, consumer insight and portraits. In collaboration with Added Value, she produced award-winning insights on Chinese consumers. She's travelled extensively in China, Brazil and other locations to photograph images for the BrandZ™ reports. Her photographs of China have been exhibited in the Houses of Parliament, London. In collaboration with Danish book publisher Politikens Forlag, she's photographed travel books about India, Greece and Denmark, her native country.

THE HISTORY
OF RETAIL IN
100 OBJECTS

www.retail100objects.com

Sources

In addition to the expertise, judgement, experience and observations of the contributing team, the following have been used as references, cross-references or sources.

WEBSITES

adage.com
adventuresintheprinttrade.blogspot.co.uk
arts.cultural-china.com
Boston Business Journal
edisontechcenter.org
emerging-advertising-media.wikispaces.com
en.parisinfo.com
en.wikipedia.org
Europe Viewed Through American Spectacles
(Google books), Charles Carroll (1874)
European Business Review 23
faculty.quinnipiac.edu
graphicdesign.about.com
homepage.ntlworld.com
idowindows.wordpress.com
inventors.about.com
labellevitrine.blogspot.co.uk
library.thinkquest.org
mntr.babcdn.com
ohioline.osu.edu
packagingrevolution.net
pasystemhistory.blogspot.co.uk
plasticsmakeitpossible.com
qrcodescanning.com
retailindustry.about.com
russiapedia.rt.com
sarahmarie1.hubpages.com
StoreBrandsDecisions.com
style.selfridges.com
The Interior Design Body of Knowledge by Martin
and Guerin
'Three-Dimensional Branding' by Herman Miller.
usedstepvan.com
Venice: Its Individual Growth from the Earliest
Beginnings to the Fall of the Republic, Horatio
Forbes Brown. (Google books).
wcfcourier.com
What Is Branding? by Matthew Healey
www.1900s.org.uk
www.allen-signs.co.uk
www.aluminium-cans.com.au
www.aluminum.org
www.ancestry.com
www.archaic-jade.com
www.articlesbase.com

www.averyweigh-tronix.com
www.aviewoncities.com
www.batleys.co.uk
www.bbc.co.uk
www.bos.frb.org
www.bpf.co.uk
www.brickhousesecurity.com
www.britannica.com
www.britishmuseum.org
www.cctvsystems.com
www.chiddingstone.kent.sch.uk
www.chinese-traditions-and-culture.com
www.coca-cola.co.uk
www.computerhistory.org
www.connectionnewspapers.com
www.creditcards.com
www.datamars.com
www.departmentstorehistory.net
www.designboom.com
www.destination360.com
www.detail-online.com
www.displayarama.com
www.economist.com
www.ee.ryerson.ca
www.ehow.com
www.elect-mer.com
www.englishforeveryone.org
www.EzineArticles.com
www.fundinguniverse.com
www.guardian.co.uk
www.historyofpa.co.uk
www.hoistmagazine.com
www.hostmerchantservices.com
www.ideafinder.com
www.italyguides.it
www.lift.co.uk
www.livescience.com
www.livinglanguage.com
www.managementstudyguide.com
www.moah.org
www.nationalcareersservice.direct.gov.uk
www.nationalgasmuseum.org.uk
www.neonlab.com
www.old.readrussia.com
www.panoston.com

www.pinnaclejournals.com
www.popularmechanics.com
www.radio-electronics.com
www.recycling.com
www.scribd.com
www.searsarchives.com
www.shirebooks.co.uk
www.squidoo.com
www.stevens.edu
www.stormshock.com
www.telegraph.co.uk
www.tescopoly.org
www.theatlantic.com
www.thecalculatorsite.com
www.thehistoryoftelevision.com
www.themhedajournal.org
www.todayifoundout.com
www.ttt-services.co.uk
www.tupperwarecollection.com
www.ukfinancialoptions.co.uk
www.vendingmachine.co.uk
www.warpaths2peacepipes.com
www.waterstones.com
www.wired.com
www.wisegeek.com
www.worldshipping.org
www.zdnet.com

OTHER

The story of the intel chip courtesy
of the Intel Corporation Museum

Index
of Objects

THE HISTORY OF RETAIL

FUTURE OBJECTS

PODCAST SERIES
Download the entire series FREE.

Includes additional stories for each of the 100 Objects.

Go to iTunes and search for 'The History of Retail 100' or go to www.retail100objects.com

SCAN WITH
layar